Girl Talk

Nicole O'Dell

with daughters Natalie & Emily

BARBOUR
PUBLISHING

ISBN 978-1-61626-557-1
eBook Editions:
Adobe Digital Edition: (.epub) 978-1-60742-762-9
Kindle and MobiPocket Edition: (.prc) 978-1-60742-763-6

The author is represented by MacGregor Literary.

Scripture quotations marked AMP are taken from the Amplified® Bible, © 1954, 1958,1962, 1964, 1965, 1987 by The Lockman Foundation. Used by permission.

Scriptures marked ASV are taken from the American Standard Version of the Bible.

Scripture quotations marked CEV are from the Contemporary English Version, Copyright © 1991, 1992, 1995 by American Bible Society. Used by permission.

Scripture quotations marked ESV are from The Holy Bible, English Standard Version®, copyright © 2001 by Crossway Bibles, a publishing ministry of Good News Publishers. Used by permission. All rights reserved.

Scripture marked GNT taken from the Good News Translation—Second Edition, Copyright © 1992 by American Bible Society. Used by permission.

Scripture marked GW is taken from *GOD'S WORD®,* © 1995 God's Word to the Nations. Used by permission of Baker Publishing Group. All rights reserved.

Scripture quotations marked KJV are taken from the King James Version of the Bible.

Scripture quotations marked MSG are from *THE MESSAGE.* Copyright © by Eugene H. Peterson 1993, 1994, 1995, 1996, 2000, 2001, 2002. Used by permission of NavPress Publishing Group.

Scripture quotations marked NASB are taken from the New American Standard Bible, © 1960, 1962, 1963, 1968, 1971, 1972, 1973, 1975, 1977, 1995 by The Lockman Foundation. Used by permission.

Scripture quotations marked NIV are taken from the HOLY BIBLE, NEW INTERNATIONAL VERSION®. NIV®. Copyright ©1973, 1978, 1984, 2011 by Biblica, Inc.™ Used by permission. All rights reserved worldwide.

Scripture quotations marked NKJV are taken from the New King James Version®. Copyright © 1982 by Thomas Nelson, Inc. Used by permission. All rights reserved.

Scripture quotations marked NLT are taken from the *Holy Bible.* New Living Translation copyright © 1996, 2004, 2007 by Tyndale House Foundation. Used by permission of Tyndale House Publishers, Inc. Carol Stream, Illinois 60188. All rights reserved.

Published by Barbour Publishing, Inc., P.O. Box 719, Uhrichsville, Ohio 44683, www.barbourbooks.com

Our mission is to publish and distribute inspirational products offering exceptional value and biblical encouragement to the masses.

 Member of the
Evangelical Christian
Publishers Association

Printed in the United States of America.
Versa Press, East Peoria, IL 61611-9788; January 2012; D10003109

Introduction

I'm Nicole O'Dell, the author of the popular Scenarios for Girls interactive fiction series and the host of Teen Talk Radio, as well as a mom of six. I, along with my daughters, Emily and Natalie, host an advice column at my website, www.nicoleodell.com, called Girl Talk. Readers write in with their tough dilemmas about life, character, body image, fashion, friendship, boys, choices, and family, and we offer them trustworthy, biblical advice.

In this book, you'll find 180 questions along with answers and related scriptures that will both encourage and challenge you in your faith walk. We've included some of the questions we've posted on the website, but most of the ones you'll read in this book are brand new. They're all actual questions from real girls who have struggled with tough issues.

Have questions about life stuff—relationships, character, body image, fashion, gossip. . . ? Look no further!

This book is for all of you awesome readers who have trusted us
with your problems and needs. Every page in this book represents
a real family or a real teen with trials and struggles that reach dozens
more smack-dab in the middle of their own realities. Thank you all
for baring your hearts and trusting us to offer a solution to your deepest
and darkest battles, and then allowing us to share it with others
who might be going through the same thing.

Acknowledgments

Carolyn Charz, aka Mom, aka Grandma Party, thanks so much for your help! Your scripture searches and verifications helped us a ton. Thanks for bouncing around thoughts and ideas, too. You're the best!

Debra Lee, Cassie Beck, Cara Putman, Cindy Thomson, Julie Higgins, and Cheryl Eklund—thanks for going off in search of teens-with-questions for us. Your responses to my call for help were so greatly appreciated.

Thank you, too, to all of the readers, Tweeters, and Facebookers who have written in with questions for the Girl Talk column and for this book. Thanks for letting us use your dilemmas to help other girls.

We also owe a big thank-you to our Savior, Lord, and Divine Counselor, Jesus Christ. You're the answer to our deepest need and the solution to our greatest dilemma.

Contents

BFFS AND NOT-SO-BFFS

BFF (Or Not?)

Q: *I always seem to pick bad friends. We end up fighting, or they turn out to be liars or backstabbers. I just had one friend—my new best friend this year—steal my other best friend from me. Now they just sit somewhere and whisper and giggle about me all the time. What would you do? And how do I know who to trust and be friends with?*

~STEPHANIE

NATALIE: I think you should first ask them if you hurt them somehow so you can try to fix it. If not, then let go and meet new people. The best way I know to pick the right kind of friends is to explore a little and give it time. Instead of calling one person your best friend after a couple of weeks of hanging out together, you should take time getting to know her and make sure you share the same values and have lots of things in common.

NICOLE: Stephanie, I think your last question is the one you really need to ask, so I'll get to that in a second. But first, you asked for advice about what to do. Honestly, don't do anything until you pray about it. Without God's help, your choices are to fight back or cry in a corner. With His help you can be strong and move on, confident and secure. You can pray for the girls and ask the Lord to convict their hearts about the way they've treated you. But otherwise, they aren't the kind of girls you want to be friends with anyway.

Which you know. Which is why you asked the last question.

One way you can tell who might be a good friend and someone you can trust is by finding out how she feels about God. Does she go to church? Does she come from a good family that teaches her values and morals? Does she care about pleasing God? If the answer to those questions is yes, then there's a good chance she's a good person. That doesn't mean she'll be perfect—but neither are you, right? It does mean that she has a foundation, something to help her know what's right and how to act.

Give all your worries and cares to God, for he cares about you.
1 PETER 5:7 NLT

I Saw Him First!

Q: *My friend and I are in sixth grade and we both like the same guy. I don't want our friendship to end because of this. What should I do?*

~KEZIA

NATALIE: I wasn't allowed to date or have a "boyfriend" at your age. In fact, I'm thirteen and I'm still not allowed to. Looking back, I think I agree with my parents and can see why they want me to wait. I think it's more important to focus on your friendships—not just the one with your friend who likes the same guy, but all of your friends. Those are the relationships that will last. They're the ones that are important.

About both of you liking the same guy, you can use that to make your friendship stronger. If your friend realizes that you were willing to set those feelings aside because she was more important to you, she'll know just how much you care about her. Friendships have the chance of lasting your whole life, but no boyfriend you have now is still going to be your boyfriend when you're older.

NICOLE: Ah. Been there. When I was just a little bit older than you, I got into one of these situations with a friend of mine. I chose the boy, and I still regret it today. Over twenty years later I wonder how much that choice hurt her and how much my stupid

actions impacted her teen years. It's not something I'm proud of, that's for sure, and I would change my choice if I could.

Natalie is so right that your friendship can last forever, but your early teen crushes are not going to follow you through life. My advice to you when it comes to things like this: *run*. Run as far as you can away from any conflict over a boy. Hug your friend, and thank God for her.

> *A friend is always loyal.*
> PROVERBS 17:17 NLT

Leave It to Beaver

Q: *My mom and dad love my best friend. They're always talking about how great she is—how smart, how nice, how good. But she really isn't the good girl they think she is. Among other things, she drinks alcohol sometimes and got in trouble for stealing about a year ago. Should I tell them or just let them keep thinking that they wished I were more like her? But if I tell them, they might either think I'm making it up or, worse, make me stop hanging around her! What should I do?*

~TRISHA

EMILY: This is a tough one. It kind of depends on what your goal is. Are you worried about your friend because she's doing bad things and you want to help her do the right things? Or are you more bothered that your parents think she's better than you? If it's really that you're worried about her, you should talk to your parents and to her. If it's just that you don't want your parents to think she's better than you, then you should have a talk with your mom and dad about why you think they feel that way.

NICOLE: There was a TV show back in my day called *Leave It to Beaver*. On it Eddie Haskell was Wally Cleaver's best friend, and he put on the same kind of snow job it sounds like your friend does and really had the parents fooled. But deep down, even though he was a player, I believed Eddie Haskell had a big heart, and insecurity drove his actions.

It's hard to say why your friend feels the need to put on false pretenses with people. Or why she acts the way she really does—the alcohol, stealing, etc. But it sounds to me like she needs help. Those things are dangerous, not only for her, but for you, too. You need to be honest with your parents and let them decide how to handle it. They'll probably be shocked, and they might make you stop hanging out with her for a while. Whatever happens, they'll know what to do.

> *If someone is trapped in sin, you should gently lead that person back to the right path. But watch out, and don't be tempted yourself.*
> GALATIANS 6:1 CEV

Boundaries

Q: *I'm a nice person. I try to be friends with everyone. I usually stand up for someone who's getting picked on or teased. I never, ever reject someone's friendship just because other people think that person isn't popular enough or cool enough. The problem is, sometimes I attract some rather annoying kids who want to be my best friends. They follow me everywhere and call me all the time. I don't want to be rude, but I'd like some space. How can I get them to loosen up a little?*

~VIOLET

EMILY: You might have to speak up and ask that they give you a little more space. Are there other people you could maybe introduce them to so they have more friends and don't need to spend all of their time with you?

One of my best friends likes to be my partner in everything we do. I'd like to partner with other kids sometimes, too, but she gets sad about it. I still do what I know is right and best for me by having more than just a few friends. I think it's okay to stand up for yourself and not let other people's moods control you.

NICOLE: First of all, Violet, I commend you for treating people kindly no matter how unpopular they are. You're right, though: you don't need to be everyone's best friend—it would be impossible, and you have the right to select whom you develop those close bonds with.

Boundaries are simply that. They just define what's okay with you and what isn't. Say something like, "I value our friendship and love the time we spend together. I think it's reasonable for us to talk on the phone two to three times a week and hang out once a week. But I need to have space so I can have other friendships, too." It's kind but leaves no room for misunderstanding. Sometimes it's difficult to confront issues like this, but it's always worth it. Keep being the great person you are, but take care of yourself, too.

A man of too many friends comes to ruin, but there is a friend who sticks closer than a brother.
PROVERBS 18:24 NASB

Sticks and Stones

Q: *How should I deal with being bullied when it's my friends who are bullying me? I have two friends, supposedly my best friends, who pick on me all the time but act like they're just kidding. Some of the things they say really hurt me. Since they laugh it off, am I being too sensitive?*

~KATIE

EMILY: My first thought is that it's hard to imagine you'd call these people your friends if they're bullying you. I think either they're jealous of you and want to put you down, or they see you as an easy target and think they look cool if they pick on you. Either way, that's not how a friend behaves. It's time to pull away from them and make some new friends. Don't you think?

NICOLE: Yeah, I can't see myself identifying these girls as my friends, either. Bullying, peer pressure, teasing, taunting, mocking, etc., are all behaviors that show a lack of love or friendship. They come, like Em said, from jealousy, pain, anger, and other motivations that are opposite of respect and support—qualities in a good friendship. By laughing off your hurt, they're showing coldness to pain they're causing you, which is even worse than the bullying itself.

If I were you, I'd just pull away. Don't try to change them or even convince them you're right. Just shrug and walk away. Show them that what they do or say has no effect on you. It will make them crazy mad if they can't get a rise out of you, but eventually either they'll move on to picking on someone else, or they'll apologize. Either way, you win.

I call upon the Lord, who is worthy to be praised, and I am saved from my enemies.
PSALM 18:3 ESV

Plant a Seed

Q: *How do I witness to my friends when they seem to have answers against everything I believe? Sometimes I think I'd do more good if I just kept my mouth shut and let them believe what they want to. What should I do?*

~CHERIE

NATALIE: I think it's awesome that in this world full of all this garbage, you're trying to share Jesus with your friends. One good way to start is to pray for guidance and wisdom from God so your point will be understood. It's good to have a few verses in your heart that you can share, but you definitely don't have to know everything before you try to share your faith. If people have questions about what you're saying or if you get confused, it's okay to say you need to find the answer and get back to them. Then ask for help and pray for wisdom.

NICOLE: I've had those conversations before—the ones where it seems like the other person always has an answer to combat everything I'm saying. Even though it's frustrating, you just have to press on. You might not see results at that moment, but over time, you may see that you were the one who planted a seed. Later on, maybe even years later, someone else might come along and water that seed. Still someone else might get to actually cultivate it to maturity.

Also, put yourself in the other person's shoes. What if the person who has an answer for everything could say the same thing about you? What if her beliefs are just as important to her as yours are to you? Can you see that she might feel attacked? It's important that you always handle these conversations with love. That's easier to do when you remember that you're representing Jesus to the people you're witnessing to, and you aren't responsible for their reactions—let the Holy Spirit handle that.

> *But dedicate your lives to Christ as Lord. Always be ready to defend your confidence in God when anyone asks you to explain it. However, make your defense with gentleness and respect.*
> 1 PETER 3:15 GW

Through Thick and Thin

Q: My friend has cancer and it's really bad. We're only seventeen. I just can't stand the thought that she might not make it. What can I do to help her?

~MELIKA

NATALIE: The most important thing you can do with her and for her is to pray. Help her feel like she's making memories and don't dwell on the sickness. Find things she's able to do so she doesn't feel like life is over. Scrapbooking is a great idea of something you can do together to remember the happy moments in life. Things like fund-raisers and awareness campaigns are good ways to help her feel loved.

NICOLE: I'm so sorry that you're going through this with your friend. I'm praying for her and for you. In order to really help your friend, a few things come to mind:

Listen: Be ready to offer her a shoulder to cry on, or a listening ear when she's frustrated or angry.

Pray: Pray for her and with her. Let her know about the faith you have in God and that you're covering her in prayer every single day.

Ask: Come right out and ask her how you can help her. Tell her you're not sure what she needs, but that you want to be the best friend you can be.

Most importantly, don't hide from your friend or ignore the situation. Many times, teens in your situation will run from the reality of serious illness or the potential of death and bury themselves in normal teenage activities to try to dull the pain and confusion. While that's a natural response, you need to fight against it for your friend's sake and for your own.

More than anything, she needs to know that you understand the seriousness of what she's going through and that you're standing beside her. Make her a priority.

Many continued prayers!

A friend always loves, and a brother is born to share trouble.
PROVERBS 17:17 GW

A Heart Change

Q: *I have a friend who's starting to do bad things, and I want her to stop. How do I stand up to her without making her mad?*

~PAULA

EMILY: If she gets mad when you're only trying to help her, she might not be a great friend. You should really try hard to get her to listen. You'll probably be surprised at how she reacts. Maybe no one has tried to tell her the right path to take and you'll be saving her from some big mistakes.

NICOLE: Yeah, it's important to be willing to stand up for truth even if people get upset with you. You never know what her reaction will be, as Emily said. Maybe she'll have more respect for you and follow your lead. Maybe she'll end her friendship with you. There's no way to know. Whatever she does, you, as a Christian who's aware, have a calling to speak up about God and His ways.

However, you have to remember that as a Christian, you're going to hold yourself to higher standards because you've decided to walk with Jesus. If your friend hasn't made that choice, then she has a different set of values than you and may not see things as wrong the same way you do. The key to changing her behaviors is in helping her change her heart, not just her mind. No matter how good she is or how bad she is, if she doesn't have Jesus, it won't matter in the end. Live as a great example of the love of Christ in her life, not just an example of good behavior, and work harder to win her for Jesus than to get her to do the right thing. Her actions will follow her heart.

> *Guard your heart above all else, for it determines the course of your life.*
> PROVERBS 4:23 NLT

Pure and Blameless

Q: *My friend sleeps around. Now people think I do. How do I fix my reputation and help my friend? Jesus was a friend to all types of people—how can I still be a friend to someone I know has a "reputation," while keeping mine pure and blameless?*

~Isabella

NATALIE: The only way to truly protect your reputation is to live it consistently. It is natural for people to assume you approve of the actions of the people you hang around with the most. So, while you need to be loving and a friend to all types of people, make sure your very best friends are those who share your values.

NICOLE: Natalie and some of her friends have a video about reputation available on the Scenarios4Girls YouTube channel. You should check it out. The truth of it is, the people you hang around with do affect your reputation. You're obviously not the same people, and there's some natural division there. But just as natural is the human instinct to lump people in one category. If you're hanging around with people who do bad things, other people will naturally assume that you at least condone the behavior, if not approve of it or participate in it.

Some practical tips for being friendly with everyone but not appearing to condone bad behavior would be to maintain your own sense of style and have friends of all types. Also, don't "lol" at questionable things on Facebook, even if someone posts it on your page. Speaking of Facebook, be very careful of the status updates you post—they really affect your reputation in big ways.

The most important thing, though, is to not compromise on what you approve of. If you're with some friends who start doing something you wouldn't want people to think you participated in, leave. A good reputation is so hard to build, but so easy to lose.

> *A good name is more desirable than great riches; to be esteemed is better than silver or gold.*
> Proverbs 22:1 NIV

Walk the Talk

Q: *My best friend has started doing things with her boyfriend that I know are wrong. She's only thirteen, and I'm afraid she's going to really mess up. How can I help her to stop and slow down?*

~Myah

NATALIE: I think you should get your friend alone for a nice long talk. She needs to be separated from her boyfriend so you can really talk openly with her. I don't know how far things have gone already, but it sounds like she's already on a slippery slope. If it's gotten to the point where she could be risking pregnancy or diseases, you should show her a video or give her a book that will help her see the cost of her decisions. Be willing to involve adults like her parents, your parents, guidance counselors, or youth leaders who can help reach out to her. You're being a good friend by trying to step in and keep her from making a disastrous mistake.

NICOLE: This is really common, unfortunately, and I'm glad you're concerned about your friend rather than just following along. There are a lot of things you can tell her about purity and about waiting for sexual things until she's married as a gift to herself and her future spouse. Thirteen is way too young to start giving away her heart and body to a boyfriend, because she'll be left with nothing to share with her husband.

More important than what you say to her, though, is the walk you model in front of her. Your words won't mean anything if your actions aren't in line with them. So be sure you're committed to your own walk of purity and then talk to her about that once she has seen it evidenced in your own life.

> *God's will is for you to be holy, so stay away from all sexual sin.*
> 1 Thessalonians 4:3 NLT

Shoplifters Will Be Prosecuted

Q: *I used to suspect that my best friend steals from stores, but now I know it for sure. She's been bragging about it lately. She steals clothes, jewelry, CDs. . .anything she thinks she can get away with. It seems like it's become a game for her. What should I do?*

~Maya

NATALIE: Shoplifting is wrong, but maybe your friend doesn't realize that she's hurting someone else by what she's doing. You should make a list of all the things you know she's stolen and add up the total cost. That way you can really show her how she's affecting the people she's stealing from. At the same time, I think you need to talk to her and give her a chance to tell her parents what's been going on. The stuff needs to be returned and she needs to own up for what she's done, so it's necessary that her parents know.

NICOLE: Shoplifting is a major problem—not just the legal risks, but also the addictive qualities like you're describing. Shoplifters get a rush out of getting something for free. Sometimes they feel the world owes them because of some kind of loss they experienced. Other times they simply get a kick out of getting one over on the authorities. And it's not always about money. Sometimes it's a cry for attention or to fill a deep personal void. Have you heard of Winona Ryder? She's a famous Hollywood actress—rich, successful, beautiful—and has been accused of and/or arrested for shoplifting. She can afford to buy herself whatever she wants, yet she has been lured to the risk and rush of stealing.

In the case of your friend, this is more than a prank or a bad choice. She has a problem and needs help. It's time to go to a parent, advisor, or guidance counselor—someone who will know how to handle it and get her help, not just punishment.

> *Let the thief no longer steal,*
> *but rather let him labor,*
> *doing honest work with his own hands,*
> *so that he may have something to*
> *share with anyone in need.*
> EPHESIANS 4:28 ESV

BFF. . .Really?

Q: *What do you do when a friend gets a boyfriend and ditches you completely? And how do you try to not be upset with her or jealous that you can't spend time with her anymore because she constantly chooses him over you?*

~AMBER

EMILY: I've had this happen when friends make new friends and forget about me. It hurts, but I suggest you try to realize that situations like this are showing you what's really in her heart. You can't make her choose you over a boy, or do anything she doesn't want to do. You can only move forward and do things differently now that you know her better. This is why it's good to have more than one best friend.

NICOLE: Ah, BFFs. The concept is great until a boy comes along and gets between you, right? I think everyone deals with this at least once. It's very painful to think your best friend is choosing someone over you. Really, though, that's not what she's doing.

There's a misconception among teens that says boy/girl relationships are more important than friendships. It's a mind-set that makes it okay to abandon friendships in pursuit of a relationship. It's a hurtful thing unless you take the time to realize that your friend is just trying to find her way.

That being said, the only way to have real friends is to be one. You can kindly talk to her and let her know that what she's doing is hurting you. Ask her to consider her actions and remind her that balance is good— balancing her time and focus between the various relationships in her life rather than throwing all of her attention at one boy is the best idea.

Two are better than one, because they have a good return for their labor: If either of them falls down, one can help the other up.
ECCLESIASTES 4:9–10 NIV

Friendship Gone Wrong

Q: *I've had the same two friends for many years. Lately they've been doing some bad things and trying to get me to do them, too. I kind of want to distance myself from them, but how do you separate from bad friends without hurting them or making them think you're stuck up?*

~MINA

EMILY: This is something I go through, too. If they're mad at you or think you're stuck up, it means they aren't trying to really understand and get to know the real you. They aren't real friends anyway.

If you want to separate from those friends (which is probably a good idea), you could join a club or start a new sport—busy yourself with something other than what you normally do so you can meet new people and not always be around the same ones.

NICOLE: I really commend you, Mina, for looking at people closely and deciding from their fruits if they're good people to be around. At this time in your life, it's vital that you surround yourself with people who will encourage you in your walk with God and support good choices. You want to be as free from peer pressure as possible, and not risk your reputation by associating with people who do bad things.

Sadly, you can't control what people think all the time. These girls might think you're stuck up just so they don't have to face up to the real reason you don't want to be around them. If they recognize it's their fault, they'd have to admit they're doing wrong, and that's unlikely. But you know what? That's okay. Their reactions to your choices shouldn't determine what you do. If you follow God's leading, He'll be with you through whatever happens.

> *Don't be fooled by those who say such things, for "bad company corrupts good character."*
> 1 CORINTHIANS 15:33 NLT

Moving Away

Q: *My best friend is mad at me. She's moving away and doesn't think I'm sad about it. I don't know how to show her or tell her that I'm heartbroken. She won't listen to me! I feel wrongly accused of something, but I can't figure out how to convince her. What should I do?*

~Selena

NATALIE: The best thing you can do is to let her know how you feel, then let it wait for a while. Let her think about things and work through her feelings. She's going through a lot right now, so try to be understanding. Don't worry about it; you're not doing anything wrong, but it might take her awhile to figure things out.

NICOLE: You know what I hear in that question, Selena? Two young girls who are both very sad. Your friend's whole life is changing and she's not able to stop it or control any of what happens to her. Sometimes when people go through things like that, they don't know how to handle their emotions and react to things in strange ways.

A move is a huge step and she's worried about a lot of things—meeting new people, making new friends, starting at a new school, etc. She's probably a little jealous that you get to stay behind and don't have to go through any of that, and she assumes that her move doesn't matter to you as much as it does to her. That's natural, obviously, but it's still difficult for her to face. Showing her grace and understanding while she goes through this tough time is the best way you can be a good friend to her even when she's acting silly.

> *A friend loves at all times, and a brother is born for a time of adversity.*
> **Proverbs 17:17 niv**

THE SKINNY ON BODY IMAGE

Are You Going to Eat That?

Q: *I have a friend who is pretty skinny, but she thinks she's fat. She is always on a diet, and I actually heard her make herself throw up in the school bathroom a couple of times. I think she looks sick, and she is just wasting away to nothing. What should I do about it? Or is it none of my business?*

~SASHA

NATALIE: You definitely need to talk to a school counselor or an adult you trust. This isn't something you can mess around with. Bulimia and anorexia can lead to death and other very harmful situations. Did you know she could damage her body to where she can't have children or could suffer other lifelong side effects? You could also show her a picture of herself and let her know that you think she's beautiful, but that she looks unhealthy. Also, you can try to stick close to her for a while so she doesn't have the opportunity to make herself throw up. Hopefully, in the meantime, you'll be able to get some adults involved who will get her the help she needs.

NICOLE: Thanks so much for writing to us, Sasha. You know, it's a tough thing to get involved in because it's hard to know what the end result will be. The first step, as in most things, should be to talk to your friend openly and honestly. Let her know how worried you are and why. Arm yourself with the facts.

Also, I did a radio show about this issue. You can check it out by searching the Teen Talk Radio podcasts on iTunes to hear real-life stories from women who suffered with an eating disorder as a teenager.

After you've done your homework and had a good talk with your friend, if things don't change, you've got to take more drastic measures. Your friend's health and even her life are at stake. You can go to a guidance counselor or go straight to her parents. I'm praying for your friend and for your strength and wisdom as you reach out to her.

Do you not know that your body is a temple of the Holy Spirit within you, whom you have from God?
1 CORINTHIANS 6:19 ESV

Double Zero

Q: *I'm sixteen and I'm 106 pounds as of this morning. I'm active—cross-country and track—and I exercise every day that I don't have practice. My parents are always trying to get me to eat more, but I don't want to gain weight—it'll mess up my sports. Plus, my track coach has hinted that he'd like me to lose a few more pounds. What should I do?*

~LEILA

NATALIE: Sometimes when I look in the mirror, I see something that isn't really the truth. But when I see pictures, I see what everyone else sees. So maybe you could take some current pictures and really try to look at yourself and see yourself the way other people do. That way, you can get a better idea of your true size.

If your parents want you to eat more, maybe you should just change what you eat. It would make your parents happy to see you eat more and you wouldn't gain weight if you eat the right things like vegetables, fruit, salad, and fat-free yogurt. And drink water or milk instead of pop.

NICOLE: The key sentence I grabbed onto in your question, Leila, was that your parents are always trying to get you to eat more. They're worried—that tells me all I need to know. The exercise is fine, the sports are great, and watching what you eat is a healthy idea, too. The problem comes in when you let your body get depleted—sounds to me like that's what your parents are worried about.

Some of the warning signs of an eating disorder include:

- Unnatural concern about body weight (even if the person is not overweight)
- Obsession with calories, fat grams, and food
- Use of any medicines to keep from gaining weight
- Throwing up after meals
- Refusing to eat or lying about how much was eaten
- Fainting
- Over-exercising
- Not having periods
- Increased anxiety about weight
- Denying that anything is wrong

Any of those things is cause for concern, so I posted them here so you can take a hard look at what's going on.

Feed me with the food that is needful for me: lest I be full, and deny thee, and say, Who is Jehovah?
PROVERBS 30:8–9 ASV

Dangerous Ground

Q: *My friend says I have an eating disorder. I really don't think I do. I'm a size two, but some of my friends are a zero or even smaller—so it's not like I'm the skinniest one. I eat dinner with my family every day. I don't ever eat breakfast, but most of my friends don't either. Sometimes I eat lunch, sometimes I don't. Every once in a while, I eat a lot of stuff that I don't usually eat, and then I make myself throw up. But it's not like I do that every day or even every week. I really don't think it's a problem. Do you?*

~SARA

EMILY: I think the best idea would be for you to talk to your mom or dad, or someone you trust, and ask them for advice. Be sure to be honest about exactly what you eat so they know enough facts to actually help you. I haven't had this concern much yet, but I am seeing that my friends are getting worried about weight and clothes. My mom says that I shouldn't worry about it at all. She says that I'll be dealing with those issues forever, and she doesn't want me to start now. Looking at your situation, I can really understand what she means. Just love yourself for who you are, and don't worry so much about appearance.

NICOLE: Sara, what you're describing is called binging and purging. . .bulimia. I realize that you don't do that very often, but the mind-set that allows you to do it once in a while will lead you to do it more and more as you get older and naturally put on more weight as your body achieves its adult size. You're on dangerous ground with this, and your friends are very right to be concerned. Please, please, talk to your parents about this. You need to get some help now, before things get out of control.

Taste and see that the LORD is good. Blessed is the person who takes refuge in him.
PSALM 34:8 GW

27

Dumpling

Q: *I'm a little bit overweight, and my dad teases me all the time. It's not just fun teasing—he also says kind of mean things sometimes, too. Like he's always asking if the seat belt is too small yet. Who says that to his daughter? And trust me, I'm not that overweight, but I'm afraid I will be if he doesn't back off. How can I make him stop?*

~MAGGIE

NATALIE: I'm so sorry that you're dealing with this. I can't imagine how it must hurt to hear that stuff from your dad. Have you talked to him honestly about how you feel? He needs to know how much this hurts you and that you fear it's going to send you down a path of depression that will lead to weight gain.

NICOLE: That has to be very difficult. I went through many periods of being overweight in my life. I know exactly how it feels. And, interestingly enough, my dad dealt with it in much the same way. He called me "dumpling" and names that he thought were funny and cute when I was little, but really kind of stung by the time I got into middle school.

Have you talked to him about it or asked your mom to talk to him for you? Maybe he just doesn't know that his joking hurts your feelings.

In the end, though, no matter if he changes or not, it's important that you find your joy and your identity in what God thinks and says about you, not in what your dad or anyone else does. If it's not your dad saying something hurtful, it might be someone at school. Words hurt, even ones said in humor, but you can move past them if you really believe the truth about who you are in Christ, which has nothing to do with your physical appearance.

Let [your adornment] be the hidden person of the heart, with the imperishable quality of a gentle and quiet spirit, which is precious in the sight of God.
1 PETER 3:4 NASB

Just the Way You Are

Q: *I'm sixteen, and I can't stand my nose. It's huge, and I have a really small face. I'd love to have a nose job and think I might be able to get my grandma to pay for it, but I'm afraid my mom will say no. What do you think?*

~SARA

EMILY: I don't think a sixteen-year-old should surgically change her body in any way. God made you just the way He wanted to. I would be terrified of any surgery—especially one I didn't need. Do you know they have to actually break your nose for a nose job? Ouch!

NICOLE: I'm so sad that our world has become a culture that desires such perfection that a young girl would consider surgical procedures to achieve an ideal that probably only exists in her own mind. Sara, your face is still changing, as is your mind and heart. If nothing else, I beg you to wait until you're an adult to see if you still feel the way you do about your nose. Even then, I don't necessarily support it, but I'm not completely opposed as I am to the idea of a teenager surgically altering herself forever.

Do you believe that God made you? He says you're perfect and exactly how He wanted you to be. Imagine you created a sculpture for your mom and were so proud of it, you couldn't wait to give it to her, and expected she'd treasure it forever. You watch as she unwraps it and looks at it for the first time. Her face falls in disappointment. She reaches for a chisel and begins to chip away at your creation—your gift—because it wasn't lovely enough by her standards. How would you feel?

More than crafting yourself into someone else's image of a perfect face or body, you need to dig into God's Word and find out what He thinks of you already—just the way you are.

> *"The LORD doesn't see things the way you see them. People judge by outward appearance, but the LORD looks at the heart."*
> 1 SAMUEL 16:7 NLT

Shape Up

Q: *I'm trying to lose about ten pounds so I can be in good shape when I try out for the volleyball team. My friend gave me some diet pills that are supposed to make you not hungry and burn more calories. She got them right off the shelf without a doctor's prescription. That means they're okay to take, right?*

~BRITNEY

NATALIE: I don't think it's ever okay to take diet pills. Just because something is for sale doesn't mean it's healthy or safe. When you're on a volleyball team, I can tell you from my own experience that the workouts and energy required to play well will help you get into better shape. You're going to want power, agility, and endurance, so the fitness will come naturally. If you crash diet and lose a bunch of weight, you'll be skinnier but much weaker. Don't sacrifice your health when simple nutrition and exercise will do the job.

NICOLE: There are a lot of unhealthy things available for sale, and diet pills are among them. Companies that manufacture those pills are only interested in making money. If they can get you to believe those little pills are the answer to your problems, you'll buy them and use them. The manufacturers don't care that the pills are known to cause rapid heart rate, high blood pressure, and sometimes even death. They don't care that they set you up for a lifetime of yo-yo dieting and poor body image. They don't care that you most likely don't need to lose much weight in the first place. They just want your money.

The best way to lose weight at your age (and any age) is to live a healthy lifestyle of moderate eating, good choices, and regular exercise. If you make that a permanent lifestyle choice, your body will naturally become fit and trim.

> *Don't you know that your body is a temple that belongs to the Holy Spirit? The Holy Spirit, whom you received from God, lives in you. You don't belong to yourselves.*
> 1 CORINTHIANS 6:19 GW

The Weigh

Q: *My mom is constantly worried about her weight. I wish she could see how beautiful she is, but she's always so negative about herself. What can I do to help her see the truth and get her to stop worrying about it so much?*

~PIA

NATALIE: I love your name! Have you tried to talk to your mom and let her know what you really think about her? If she still can't accept the truth about herself, or still feels uncomfortable, maybe you can help her make some goals and then stick to them. Sometimes having a partner to share in the goals makes all the difference. You could run together in the mornings, go on a diet plan together, work out to videos, or take a class together.

NICOLE: Is this a secret question my daughters have slipped in here? I have to admit, Pia, I'm just like your mom. I struggle over my weight constantly and I often lose the battle. I'm also really negative about myself and have a pretty low self-image of my physical appearance. I really, really try not to let that rub off on my kids, but I'm sure it does.

I love when my girls notice a haircut or comment on a new shirt, but mostly I love it when they ask my advice about their own clothes or appearance. It reminds me that they don't think I'm totally out of touch. When they comment about how hard I work and how they wished it were easier for me, that tells me that they really do get it.

Try to help your mom out by making healthy choices around her, and support her diet as best you can. Encouraging her to cheat isn't a good thing, even though it might feel that way at the moment. It only sets her up for regret later.

Good for you for caring enough to write in about this. You remind me of two wonderful girls I know. Now go give your mama a hug!

> *Beloved, I pray that you may prosper in all things and be in health, just as your soul prospers.*
> 3 JOHN 2 NKJV

31

BOYS, BOYS, BOYS!

Be My Valentine

Q: *My boyfriend and I (both tenth graders) went to the Valentine's Day dance where you could buy a balloon and have it delivered to someone as a surprise. A teacher came toward me with three balloons tied together. I said, "Awww! That's so sweet!" to my boyfriend because I knew that would have cost him $15. Problem was, I could tell right away by the look on his face they weren't from him. I have no idea who sent them, but now my boyfriend thinks I've got something going on behind his back. Should I leave it alone or try to find out who it was so my boyfriend will believe me?*

~BETHENY

NATALIE: The anonymous delivery is no big deal—I had that happen to me this Valentine's Day, too. In my case, I got a can of pop as a "Crush gram." I'm not doing anything about it—I don't even want to know who it was from—but I did drink the pop. The problem for you, though, is that your boyfriend doesn't believe you. If he doesn't trust you, there's a deeper problem than just balloons. You should talk to him, assure him that you're trustworthy, and find out why he has trouble trusting. If he's the jealous type, run the other way!

NICOLE: I think you should ignore the balloons as if they didn't exist. Whoever sent them must know you have a boyfriend, so he can't be too interested in a faithful, committed relationship.

But I will agree with Natalie about the trust issue. If you've given your boyfriend reason not to trust you, then you need to find out if you can move past that and begin to repair your relationship. If, however, you've never given him reason to doubt you, you need to find out why he assumes the worst. One of the most difficult issues in a relationship is a lack of trust— and it rarely improves over time. If a person is jealous and controlling by nature, it usually gets worse. Whatever you do, though, don't think you'll fix him. Let him fix himself and then come back to you.

> *Now it is required that those who have been given a trust must prove faithful.*
> 1 CORINTHIANS 4:2 NIV

Hands Off

Q: *I've known a boy for a long time, and I like him a lot. The problem is that my best friend used to go out with him for like a year. She moved away over the summer, so they broke up. She says it would hurt her feelings if I went out with him, but I don't see why. She's far away—what does she expect from him? What should I do?*

~DESTINY

EMILY: I think you need to talk openly with your friend about it again. Maybe you two can decide to try it out and see how everyone feels. If she sees that you two are happy dating each other and that you both stay friends with her still, maybe she'll be okay with it. If it's meant to be, it will work out—never choose a guy over a friend, though.

NICOLE: Hi, Destiny. I love your name, and you do have a destiny, you know?

Your destiny is to walk according to God's plans for you and see the wonderful gifts He has set aside for you. Right now, it's so important to you that you date this guy, but that might not be according to God's perfect will. I'm not trying to say your feelings aren't real. But let's face it, what are the chances that you'd still be dating him a year, two years, three years from now? Look around at the college-age people you know. How many of them are still dating a high school sweetheart? Look a few years beyond that even. . . . Do you know any? But how many of them are still friends, even best friends, with the same friends they had in high school? The chance of a lasting romantic relationship that begins in high school is extremely slim. But a friendship can last forever.

> *And we know that God causes everything to work together for the good of those who love God and are called according to his purpose for them.*
> ROMANS 8:28 NLT

36

God's Timing

Q: *I'm fourteen years old, and I've liked this boy for forever it seems like. Problem is, my best friend likes him, too. I started liking him a long time before she did, but I never told her. Now, she tells everyone that she likes him. So if I try to let her know that I liked him first, she will think I made that up because I am jealous or something. But if I don't tell her, and she decides that she doesn't like him anymore, she'll think I copied off of her by going for him. What should I do?*

*~*CRYSTAL

NATALIE: There was this one guy in sixth grade—a lot of girls liked him, including me. Basically, I just kept it to myself and only told my very best friends who understood. Having a crush on a boy is different from being ready to date or have a relationship with him. I knew I was too young for any of that, so I didn't worry about it too much. I figured it would pass. . .and it did.

NICOLE: Do you really think the boy you have a crush on today is going to be your husband one day? I know it does happen, but it's very rare. Your friendship should be more important than any boy you might like. That goes both ways, though. It should be more important to both you and your friend. A true friend would appreciate and understand your honesty.

Even so, what is she going to do? Not "like" him anymore? Are you going to all of a sudden turn into a different person and start telling people that you do "like" him? Has anyone tried to find out his thoughts about all of this? Do you see what I'm saying? Just because your thoughts predate your friend's thoughts, that doesn't give you a claim over the boy. In the end, it's up to him.

*But. . .*please, please, please consider putting all of this on hold. Once you start down this path, you'll only want to keep going. There's a time much later in your life that God meant for these relationships. Don't rush it.

There is a time for everything, and a season for every activity under the heavens.
ECCLESIASTES 3:1 NIV

The Ball's in Your Court

Q: *I'm fifteen and that's part of the problem. My parents said I could date when I turned sixteen, which is only four weeks away. There's a boy I want to date—we've actually been waiting for a year for the big one-six. Next weekend there's a special event that he really wants to take me to for our first official date. My dad says no problem; it's only three weeks early. My mom says no way; those three weeks are important. Obviously, I'm on my dad's side. We all decided to leave it up to you guys to make the call. So. . .can I go on the date?*

~RYLENE

NATALIE: I can understand how agonizing the wait is. I've had to deal with the same thing over many issues. Personally, I don't think it's a big deal to go on your date three weeks early. But when I'm a mom, I'm sure I'll figure out why it is a big deal. I think the most important thing is that you respect your parents no matter what they decide.

NICOLE: Happy early birthday! I'm sorry, but I'm not going to make this decision. I'm going to let you make it. Here are some points to consider:

- Your parents set a standard for you. Sticking by it and upholding your end of that deal will only strengthen their faith in you.
- Mom and Dad are at odds with each other over this decision. You really should do everything you can to avoid being the cause of that. You should never, ever pit one against the other.

- In my house, the no wins. For example, if my husband wants to allow something and I don't, the no wins. If I want to purchase something and he doesn't, the no wins.

Other than missing out on one fun night, what does it really mean to the big picture? What will be remembered two decades from now? The date or the fact that you gave up the date to honor your parents?

Sorry I can't make this call for you, Rylene. I think it will mean much more if you make it yourself—either way. Let us know what you decide, okay?

Children, obey your parents in everything, for this pleases the Lord.
COLOSSIANS 3:20 NIV

Boys Will Be Boys

Q: *I like hanging out with guys. They're way more fun than girls, and there's so much less drama most of the time. But it seems like it always leads to one of my boy friends liking me as more than a friend. How can I be just friends with boys without them starting to like me?*

~WENDY

EMILY: It's probably best if you try to ignore it and keep being yourself. The boys aren't doing anything wrong by liking you—I'm sure they have good reasons for it! But that doesn't mean you have to respond to it and like them back. You can be honest about how you feel, and keep being their friend.

NICOLE: I'm sure you're right, Em. The boys probably can't help themselves, Wendy! I'm sure you're a special girl and the more they get to know you, the more attractive you seem to them. So don't fault them for picking up on your good qualities. To answer your question, though, honesty works best. It's difficult to have these types of conversations with a boy, especially when you think it might hurt his feelings. But it's far better to be up front and honest than to let him hope for a relationship that you don't plan to develop with him.

Taking that a step further, let me encourage you to wait for any boy/girl relationships. You have a long road ahead of you and there's no need to spend all of it going back and forth between headache and heartache. You're off to a good start by not falling for every guy who pays attention to you, so keep up the good work and wait for that someone special God has set aside just for you.

> *A man who has friends must himself be friendly, but there is a friend who sticks closer than a brother.*
> PROVERBS 18:24 NKJV

Back for More

Q: *One thing I always have wondered is why girls let guys treat them so badly. The guy may cheat and other things, and the girl still takes him back every time.*

~Charlotte

NATALIE: You know, I never really understood that either. I just don't get why a girl would let herself get hurt over and over. Since your question asks why she does it, I've given it a lot of thought. To me, the issue comes down to self-esteem. If she doesn't feel like she's good enough for someone to treat her great, she's not going to insist on it. Also, girls like that want to be loved so badly they'll believe the promises of people who've hurt them just to have the chance to make things right.

NICOLE: Great question! Statistically, girls who let themselves get mistreated and keep coming back (or sticking around for more) are girls who haven't had a great male role model in their lives up to that point. Often they were or are currently being mistreated, belittled, or even abused by a father or stepfather. Often they want to be accepted and approved of so badly, they subconsciously look for a similar relationship with a boy in hopes of winning him over.

Also, girls in that situation often have very low self-esteem. If they think they aren't worthy of being treated well, they won't demand it for themselves.

If you know someone who is in a relationship like that, do your best to help build her self-esteem by pointing out her great qualities. You can even point out what you see happening, because she may not even realize it herself.

> *Love does not delight in evil but rejoices with the truth. It always protects, always trusts, always hopes, always perseveres.*
> 1 Corinthians 13:6–7 NIV

Wave the Red Flag

Q: *I was just wondering if you could tell me what to look for in a boy I might want to date. And what are some big red flags that I should watch out for?*

~JEN

NATALIE: Red flags for me would be if he isn't a Christian and if he's mean to people who aren't his friends. I imagine I'll also pay attention to the kind of family life he has and how he talks to his parents. When it comes time for me to date, I want to be around someone who is liked by everyone and who genuinely has a good time for the right reasons.

NICOLE: Sure! It's easy really. He should clearly love the Lord, his mom, and himself. Loving the Lord means he does his best to follow God's Word and live a godly life. He should be a praying person who seeks God's heart on issues that come up and decisions he must make. Loving his mom means he puts others first and respects his parents. Loving himself requires that he live a healthy, moderate life, free from bad choices like alcohol and drug use or reckless driving.

If he passes all of those hurdles, then you need to watch and see how he treats you. Does he treat you like a lady or like a buddy? You want to date someone who upholds you as the princess you are, but counsels you with godly expectations and righteous standards.

The opposite of any of those things is a red flag you should watch out for. And it shouldn't be a "best two out of three" scenario. When dating, you should demand it all and not take the least of the evils just because those are your only choices. God wants to fulfill that perfect list in His timing, because you're worth it. Prove you're worth it by waiting for it.

> *Do not be conformed to this world, but be transformed by the renewal of your mind, that by testing you may discern what is the will of God, what is good and acceptable and perfect.*
> ROMANS 12:2 ESV

41

Pillar of Salt

Q: *Is it wrong to want to go on a mission trip just because my boyfriend is going? I'll still do the work and be a help there, but I'm not really going because of any spiritual reason. God won't strike me dead with lightning or turn me to salt, will He?*

~ERIN

EMILY: I'm kind of neutral on this. I mean, it's not a horrible thing to do something like that just because your boyfriend is. On the other hand, it would be better if you were going because you wanted to reach people with God's grace and love. Hopefully, when you do go, and you should, you'll find the true purpose of the trip.

NICOLE: Well, it seems you know a bit of your Bible history, and that's great. I'm intrigued that you would ask this question. It shows a lot of insight into your own motivations. Many people don't have such a grasp on why they do what they do.

Honestly, I think a lot of people go on mission trips for various reasons, and most of them come home changed. They realize while they're there serving the needy and reaching out to the unloved and unchurched that there's a bigger thing going on in this world than their own little schemes or ambitions.

Okay, so you go just because your boyfriend's going. So what? Just go. I promise you'll be glad you did, and no lightning will strike you down. Oh, and from the sounds of things, I like your choice in guys.

> *And do not forget to do good and to share with others, for with such sacrifices God is pleased.*
> HEBREWS 13:16 NIV

Brokenhearted

Q: *My first boyfriend broke up with me after over a year of being together. It hurts so bad. Why wasn't I good enough for him? Will I ever find someone like him again? How do you get over a broken heart?*

~CORA

NATALIE: Surround yourself with people you love and remember that God's love is far greater than anyone else's. Let Him fill the hole in your heart.

NICOLE: There's a reason why all of those country songs are about breakups; we've all been through it and can relate to the pain in the lyrics because we have experienced it. I don't want to be trite and say something like, "This too will pass," or "You'll get over it in time." Those things are true, but I know they don't help you now.

You didn't mention how old you are, but I'm going to assume that, as a reader of mine, you're not out of high school yet. If that's the case, honey, just turn your focus onto something worthwhile. Join a team or club, rekindle a friendship, start a new hobby— just move on. Don't let this boy have this much power over your life; he obviously isn't worth it.

If there's anything you can take from this experience, be sure to do that. By that I mean listen to the reasons for the breakup and learn from what went wrong. Were you dating the wrong kind of guy? Were you too clingy?

Were you too flirty? Was he not committed? You want to learn so you can avoid mistakes in the future. Often, when girls don't really take these lessons to heart, they wind up dating the exact same guy (proverbially) again and again in a subconscious effort to get it right.

Put your hope and trust in God, and let Him be your primary relationship. Learn about yourself, how to love, and how to be loved, through *Him*.

He heals the brokenhearted and binds up their wounds.
PSALM 147:3 NIV

PDA

Q: *I'm only ten years old. Is it okay for me to hold hands with a boy? I really like him a lot!*

~EMMY

EMILY: In my opinion, definitely not. I'm around your age, and I think it would be impossible for me to know all I need to know about dating, and I don't just want to do physical stuff with guys when I'm not ready. My mom talks to me and my sister about purity all the time, but I know most girls my age aren't even aware of what that is. Holding hands is just a first step. Then what? Kissing? No. Ten is way too young for physical things that will only build on each other and lead to more. Over time, that can only cause problems as you get into more serious relationships and want more and more.

NICOLE: Hi, Emmy. I love your name—that's what I often call my Emily. Anyway, about your question, it all depends. There is nothing wrong with holding hands in itself, but I completely agree with Emily about the progression of the physical steps. Can you tell we talk about that a lot in our home?

When you like a boy, it's natural to want to have contact with him in some way. The scary part is that every time you have that contact, you're going to want it to be more meaningful. Even scarier is that, at ten years old, you have so many years left before you'll be ready for marriage. It's much better to wait a long time before giving in to those physical desires by starting the physical stuff now. Also, any kind of contact like that is definitely wrong if your parents have forbidden it, so you need to find out what they think about it, too.

Whatever you do in word or deed, do all in the name of the Lord Jesus, giving thanks through Him to God the Father.
COLOSSIANS 3:17 NASB

God's Willpower

Q: *I know you're not allowed to date, Natalie, but how do you keep yourself from being interested in a guy?*

~April

NATALIE: Um, I'd like to say I do that perfectly and never have a problem with it, but it wouldn't be true. I read my mom's answer before I wrote mine and I totally agree with her. I do have interest in boys from time to time. It's natural. I just choose not to act on it right now. As I get older, it gets a little more interesting because I might like someone who likes me back. If he doesn't have the same restrictions I do, it gets a little awkward. On the other hand, it's a good way for me to really find out if he'd respect my limits later on.

NICOLE: I don't think Natalie does keep herself from being interested. She has had very few interests over the past years—at least that I know of— but she doesn't act on them. Slowly, over time and with careful dialogue, we've lightened some of the restrictions where it seems appropriate. For example, she is now allowed to receive text messages from certain boys, with prior approval, and only with my inspection. I check her messages before she deletes them.

She is still not allowed to pair up with a boy and call him her boyfriend, or go out on actual dates except for school dances, and it will continue that way for several years. As long as Natalie continues to show the maturity of wise choices as she has so far, she'll be allowed to date when she turns sixteen.

But none of that has anything to do with interest. Sometimes you just can't help what your mind does. That's why it's not temptation that's wrong; it's acting upon it that's wrong. Having a crush on a boy, or having boys interested in her, changes nothing about our expectations for her choices and what she's allowed to do. And, so far, she's very receptive to those guidelines and respectful of my wishes.

Listen to advice and accept instruction, that you may gain wisdom in the future.
PROVERBS 19:20 ESV

45

Missionary Dating

Q: *I like a boy who isn't a Christian, and my mom won't let me go out with him. I don't think that's right. Even Jesus hung out with sinners, and maybe I'll be able to point him in the right direction. What do you think?*

~Carmen

NATALIE: My mom has said a lot to me about missionary dating—dating someone with the hopes of leading him to Christ. In the Bible it says not to be unequally yoked, which is when two cows are bound together so they can share the workload. If those cattle are unequal in strength, they won't be able to do the work their master wants them to do. The same thing is true for a Christian dating an unbeliever. Being in a relationship like that, the Christian won't be able to fully live the way God has called her to. When two people with different beliefs try to blend, the priorities get messed up. A Christian's priority is to love God with all your heart. But a non-Christian doesn't share those priorities at all.

NICOLE: Yeah, we've dealt with this a little bit in our home and it's tough to draw a line, but it's also necessary for parents to lead their teens down the right path. Teenagers, by their very nature, are not yet spiritually mature on their own walk—they're learning, growing, and being molded into who God wants you to be. Other than being a witness and a role model, it's not the time in your life to try to mentor someone else along at the expense of risking your own heartache.

Dating is a challenging and risky time. Your mom is only trying to minimize those risks by requiring that you spend your time with someone who shares your values. Rather than fight her on it, why don't you pray about it and see if you find that she's right? Then you can make the choice for yourself and show that you're well on your way through the maturing process.

> *Don't team up with those who are unbelievers. How can righteousness be a partner with wickedness? How can light live with darkness?*
> 2 Corinthians 6:14 NLT

Mixed Message

Q: *Our youth pastor tells the guys not to date till they are ready to court a girl with the intention of getting married, and he tells us girls not to date a non-Christian. We are ready to date, but the Christian guys don't want to date us yet. What is a Christian girl to do?*

~TORRIE

NATALIE: I think it's great that the boys want to wait. Usually it's the other way around. You should really show these awesome boys respect by honoring their commitment to waiting for a better time to date. One of them might be your husband one day!

NICOLE: Hmm. I kind of think you're missing the point. I don't think your youth pastor would tell the girls to go ahead and date and the boys to wait. I think he's teaching the concept of courting and expecting boys and girls alike to catch on. The girls kind of need boys in order to start dating, and if the boys are committed to waiting, then the girls have to wait, too—even if by default.

By doing it this way, he's putting boys in the leadership role of setting the standard of timing, and I like that a lot. It's closer to God's design for the family and sets the right tone for any budding courtship. Typically, in this society, if anyone is going to say no, it's the girls. They're the ones who put on the brakes or hold off on dating and physical things until they're ready. Usually (not always, of course) boys will go as far as the girls will allow, as fast as the girls will allow it. By asking boys to take responsibility for their relationships, your youth pastor is empowering them to be godly men.

Run from temptations that capture young people. Always do the right thing. Be faithful, loving, and easy to get along with. Worship with people whose hearts are pure.
2 TIMOTHY 2:22 CEV

Topsy Turvy

NATALIE: I think that in today's culture, it's most popular for the guy to ask the girl out or give the first kiss. It really helps a girl feel special and noticed. It gives any girl confidence. Besides, most girls are scared to ask the guy. I don't think there's anything necessarily wrong with it, though.

EMILY: I think it's fine for a girl to call a boy for a date. In *Magna*, by my mom, Molly called a boy to invite him to the dance. I don't think I'd agree with the girl giving the first kiss, though. Don't rush into something; really give it plenty of time.

NICOLE: I had both girls answer this because I think it's one issue that's definitely open to interpretation and personality. Personally, I couldn't ask a boy out or give a first kiss. I think, if I did, I'd always wonder if he was all that interested in me. Boys probably deal with that all the time, but they aren't typically as insecure as girls are.

I think I agree with Natalie that there's nothing definitively right or wrong with it either way, but allowing the boy to take the lead is more in line with God's design for the family unit. Besides, I'd rather see both boys and girls just wait awhile, so if you're waiting for him, and he's waiting for you. . . everybody wins!

> *He has made everything beautiful in its time.*
> Ecclesiastes 3:11 NIV

CH–CH–CH–
CHANGES

Empty

Q: *I'm about to be a junior—it's supposed to be a fun year for me. I have a car, a job, and lots of cool things to look forward to. Problem is, my three best friends and my boyfriend just graduated. Two of my friends are going far away to one college. My boyfriend and my other friend are headed just as far in the other direction to another school. I'm so frustrated and sad that I'm all alone in my junior year. It doesn't seem fair. I don't even know what I'm asking. . . .*

~ALANA

EMILY: I kind of know how you feel. Two of my good friends moved away this year. It's really hard to say good-bye. But think of it this way: at my age, it's hard to stay in touch long distance, but for you, you can call, text, e-mail, visit, drive, and anything else you can think of to stay in touch. Maybe try to focus on being happy for your friends for what they are experiencing, and then look forward to the changes you're going to have, too. I also think it might be a good time to make some new friends and meet some new people.

NICOLE: I can hear the sadness in your writing, and I'm so sorry for your loss. I'm sure it's a very difficult time for you, but sometimes change comes and even though we fight it, it turns out to be the best thing for us. I know you can't imagine anything good coming out of this, but I do want to encourage you to keep your mind, heart, and eyes open. Keep your mind open to new things and experiences. Keep your heart open to new friends. Keep your eyes open for new opportunities to grow.

And being alone a little bit now and then isn't the worst thing. Maybe the Lord wants you to get to know Him and yourself a little better.

And he said to his disciples, "Therefore I tell you, do not be anxious about your life."
LUKE 12:22 ESV

For Sale

Q: *Summer is coming, and I'm so nervous because my family is moving. I kind of want to stay behind and spend the summer with my grandparents so I can be close to my friends and then join my family later. My parents said I can do that if I want to, but they also said it might be good to spend the summer getting settled in the new home, meeting kids in the area, and learning about the town before school starts. I just don't know what to do. What would you do?*

~ALLIE

NATALIE: How about splitting it up? Half with your grandparents and half with your family? That way you can do both—spend time with your friends and have time to get to know kids in your new town. When you get to your new place, it's best to get out and get involved. Staying home and hiding just because you're nervous won't help you meet people. I think it's exciting to have the opportunity to see new places—it's all in how you look at it.

NICOLE: Moving to a new home and a new town can be such a difficult adjustment to make. It's great that your parents are willing to help make the transition as smooth as possible. I think Natalie had a great suggestion. It doesn't have to be an either/or decision—a halfway split is a good compromise and will give you the time to ease out of one place and into the other. Just remember, everything is temporary. Before you know it, you'll be giving a new student a tour of what was once your new school. Just take things one day at a time and try to find something great in each day.

> *"Be strong and courageous. Do not be afraid; do not be discouraged, for the LORD your God will be with you wherever you go."*
> JOSHUA 1:9 NIV

Something's Wrong with Me?

Q: *I learned all about having my period a long time ago, but I'm twelve and it still hasn't happened. Is that normal? I'm kind of worried.*

~LEXA

NATALIE: I don't think there's anything to worry about. At thirteen, I have several friends who either haven't started their periods yet or only very recently have. There are also some who started many years ago—long before I did. There's a wide range of normal for this, and you really shouldn't worry about it. Just be prepared for it so you're ready when it happens. You'll be dealing with hormone shifts that can cause mood swings and all sorts of fun stuff. I had no idea how it would be. It's not fun sometimes.

NICOLE: It's very normal not to have your period at twelve. Many get it sooner, and many get it slightly older. If your breasts are changing, if pubic hair is starting to develop, and if you're getting cramps in your abdomen, then you're getting close to the time when you'll start your period. It can be weeks, months, or even years from now and still be totally normal.

I recommend that you enjoy not having it and don't wish it to come sooner. It's not really a fun thing. You might experience painful cramps. You might find it to be gross and inconvenient. It makes things awkward because you always have to have feminine products with you, and your moods might be altered a bit. Plus, once it starts, you'll be dealing with it for decades.

All that to say—no rush!

> *For everything there is a season, and a time for every matter under heaven.*
> ECCLESIASTES 3:1 ESV

53

Second Chances

Q: *My parents have been divorced for a few years, and now my mom is getting remarried. I like my mom's boyfriend, but I've always hoped Mom and Dad would get back together one day. I guess there's no way that will happen now. Do you have any suggestions?*

~CHRISTINA

EMILY: My mom is remarried to my stepdad, Wil. When Mom first told me she was getting married, I got a little worried and sad because I was too young to understand it all. Now that Mom and Wil have been married for a long time, I found out that I can be happy, even with the divorce and having a stepdad. I believe that your mom would only marry someone if she knew he would be good to you and be a happy addition to your family.

Having my stepdad has been a great part of my life. We share some special things with each other, but Wil never tries to replace my dad. You should try to make your relationship with your stepdad a special one. No one can have too much love in her life.

NICOLE: I'm so sorry about the divorce, Christina, but the chances of your mom and dad getting back together were probably pretty slim even without your mom's remarriage. I'm really glad you like your soon-to-be stepdad and pray you all have a happy life together.

If you're looking for suggestions on how to get your mom and dad back together, I'm afraid I can't offer those. In this case, the best thing—and the right thing—for you to do is to respect your mom and her choices, support the family, and be respectful to those in authority—even your new stepdad. It's not his fault that the divorce happened, and truly, it's not his fault that your parents aren't getting back together. So be very careful not to take out your frustrations on him, which can happen even if you don't realize you're doing it.

Look to the LORD and his strength; seek his face always.
PSALM 105:4 NIV

Green Teen

Q: *I know I'm only a teenager, but I care about the earth. What can I do to make a difference in the environment?*

~AMBER

EMILY: I think it's really awesome that you're concerned about this. You probably know the three R's: reduce, reuse, and recycle. You can also organize some of your friends to tell people about recycling and how to make less waste in your community. Using fewer paper products and less plastic are two of the ways. You can help the earth by picking up litter if you see it on the sidewalk or the grass. You can plant trees and help them grow.

NICOLE: Great question! Just because you're a teenager doesn't mean you can't do something to help the environment. God asks us to take care of the earth, so it's important that we all do our part. There are many things you can do. Let's break down those three Rs Emily mentioned:

Reduce waste by cutting back on paper products, buying in bulk, and avoiding single-serving containers and disposable items. You can reduce energy consumption by turning off lights and adjusting the thermostat a little bit.

Reuse whenever possible. Use travel mugs instead of Styrofoam cups. If you must use plastic utensils, wash them and reuse them rather than throwing them away. Hand down clothing and other items for someone else to use. Consider used items for yourself when it's time to shop.

Recycle cans, cardboard, plastic, paper, newspaper, glass, wood, and electronics, among many other things. You can help your family participate by modeling the behavior and making it easy for them to join in. Label appropriate depositories so your family knows right where to put their recyclables.

For since the creation of the world God's invisible qualities—his eternal power and divine nature—have been clearly seen, being understood from what has been made, so that people are without excuse.
ROMANS 1:20 NIV

Opportunity Knocking

Q: *I'm about to start my first job, and I actually have two offers. I can either work at my favorite clothing store and get a great discount, or I can work at the Christian bookstore and be around Christians and good music and stuff like that all day. I love the idea of having access to all of those great clothes, but I know the Christian environment would probably be good for me. What should I do?*

~BECKY

EMILY: Would it be possible to work part-time at both places? If that weren't possible and I was faced with the same choice, I would first look at all the pros and cons, like pay, discount, scheduling flexibility, and compare them. Either way, I think as long as you're a Christian and you're following the Lord and stay close to Him, you can do whatever you think you'd enjoy more and whatever would be best for your personality.

Whichever job you chose, you'll do better at it if you really enjoy it. God is with you wherever you go, and maybe He wants you to work among non-believers so you can bring His light to others and be an example to them. You should really just pray about this and make a good decision after you pray.

NICOLE: Oh, good question. Congratulations on the awesome opportunities. As a mom, I love the idea of you working at a Christian bookstore. You'd be able to use your discount on music, books, gifts, and other fun things—plus you'd be in a great atmosphere whenever you work! I'd imagine the people you'd be around would be better influences and would share some of your beliefs and goals. Also, you'd spend far less money than if you worked in a clothing store since clothing stores usually require you to wear the latest fashions that they sell.

I really like Emily's thoughts, too, so I'm not going to tell you what to do. But if you were my daughter, I might pull rank on this one.

> *Do not conform to the pattern of this world, but be transformed by the renewing of your mind. Then you will be able to test and approve what God's will is— his good, pleasing and perfect will.*
> ROMANS 12:2 NIV

Double Duty

Q: *I'm fifteen years old. My family goes to a [certain denomination] church, but I don't like it at all! My friend goes to [a different church] that I really love, and her parents have offered to pick me up and take me with them every week. I don't think my parents should care where I go to church, as long as I go, right? But they do. They told me they'll let me go to that other church as long as I go to our family church, too—like both in the same week. What should I do?*

~Kallie

NATALIE: This is a really hard one! I tried to imagine what I would do if I were in your position. I think I'd talk to my parents. I'd probably beg. Ha-ha. But in the end, I think, at fifteen years old, I'd have to do what they thought was right.

Do you think you could make a compromise? What if you went to your family church on Sundays and then the other church for youth group and other activities? I'm sure it will work out. You won't be a teenager forever, or so I've been told.

NICOLE: Yay for a churchgoing family! I'm thrilled that your parents are raising you in the faith, and I think it's wonderful that you're taking it a step further by trying to find a place to worship that's a good fit with your personality and preferences.

Now, you might not like my answer all that much, but your religious training, at this point in your life, is your parents' responsibility. They *must* do what they believe is right. I think it's very open-minded of them to let you attend your friend's church as long as you go to your family church, too. I guess, until you're older, you'll have to decide if it's important enough for you to do that. I can't say I'd feel bad to find out you're going to double church services.

Keep searching and growing. You're doing a great job. . .and so are your parents.

Fathers, do not provoke your children to anger, but bring them up in the discipline and instruction of the Lord.
EPHESIANS 6:4 ESV

Cheeseburger Churchgoer

Q: *Why all the push to go to church? Does the Bible say a person has to go to church to be a Christian? Personally, I find it kind of boring.*

~LIZ

EMILY: Going to church doesn't make you a Christian. At church you learn about God, spend time with other Christians, and learn about what to do in your life. If you think church is boring, maybe you're not going to the right kind of church. Talk to your parents about maybe finding a different church that might interest you more. Be sure you're involved with the youth group and other fun things going on at your church.

NICOLE: Keith Green was a singer/songwriter from the 1970s. He died in a plane crash and left his book, *No Compromise*, unfinished. His wife, Melody Green, finished it for him following his death. One of the things Keith liked to say was that going to church doesn't make you a Christian any more than going to McDonald's makes you a hamburger. Being a Christian simply means you're a follower of Christ, and that is proven or disproved by the fruits in your life. Going to church can be one of those fruits if you're going there for the right reasons.

Going to church isn't a qualification for a Christian, but it is something God wants us to do. We need the time to get together with other like-minded people. We need to hear from the Word and worship God together with other believers. As Emily suggested, if you're bored at your church, you may need to look elsewhere or pray that God would show you the interesting gems in the church you attend.

We should not stop gathering together with other believers, as some of you are doing. Instead, we must continue to encourage each other even more as we see the day of the Lord coming.
HEBREWS 10:25 GW

Word Up

Q: *I really want to read my Bible every day, but I have such a hard time under-standing what it says, and I get so bored. I read and reread and just don't get anything out of it. I like the Gospels and some of the New Testament books because I understand them, but I feel like God wouldn't have made the Old Testament if He didn't want us to read it. What can I do about this?*

~Patti

EMILY: It's great that you want to know the Bible. A lot of churches have Bible studies and classes to help people learn the basics of the different parts of the Bible and how they all fit to-gether. You could attend one of those classes to get yourself off to a good start and then build from there.

NICOLE: Great suggestion, Emily. At our church, it's called Alpha, and most churches have an option like that. Even if yours doesn't, other churches are always open to visitors. Once you dig in and understand what you're reading, it might not be so boring to you. Another option is to get a transla-tion that is more in the language a teen would like to read. Teen study Bibles are available, or you could go with *The Message*.

Another option is to pick up a one-year Bible. It's organized so that you read a portion of the New Testament, a portion of the Old Testament, and a bit of Psalms or Proverbs every day. You can commit to the daily read-ings until you've made it all the way through the entire Bible in one year.

Pray as you go that God would illu-minate His truth to you and give you a good understanding of what you're reading.

> *Commit your way to the LORD;*
> *trust in him and he will do this:*
> *he will make your righteous*
> *reward shine like the dawn.*
> PSALM 37:5–6 NIV

The Whole War

Q: *My friend goes to a church that says there are many ways to heaven and that it's okay to worship whatever higher power you want to. Is that true? I thought Jesus was the only way. What can I say to her to make her see the truth?*

~Abby

NATALIE: You're right. Jesus is the only way to the Father. The Bible makes that totally clear. When other people say that you can please God by being good or working hard, reject that idea. Those things are good, definitely, but they are a response to what God has done for you, not a way to earn His favor.

NICOLE: There's an old saying that says to choose your battles, and another that says to choose which hills you're going to die on. Together, those little nuggets mean that you shouldn't argue over every little thing so when something is really important, you can fight hard for it. Your enemy would have you and your friends believe that there are many roads to God and anyone can find her own way to him (or her). But you need to fight that lie as though the entire war is over this one issue, because it is.

Jesus is the only way to the Father. It's the most important truth of the Christian faith and of the Word of God. There's no room for compromise on this issue, and that's a hill you can die on.

So flee youthful passions and pursue righteousness, faith, love, and peace, along with those who call on the Lord from a pure heart.
2 Timothy 2:22 esv

Teacher's Pet

Q: *Sometimes my teachers say things that I know are different from what the Bible says, like about evolution and stuff like that. What they say makes sense sometimes, and I think I'm beginning to believe they might be right. I don't want to because deep inside I know they're wrong. It makes me confused. What should I do?*

~Sam

EMILY: You should always follow the Bible above any other teaching. If anyone says something different than what God has said, you should talk to your parents or a youth leader and ask them to help you understand. I know there are books written just for young people to help us understand the comparison of the Bible and science. I haven't read them personally, but I've seen them around my house. I don't get it all either, but you're making me want to figure it out!

NICOLE: Emily is completely right. There is no teacher on earth—whether in your school, your church, or even your home—who can prove the Bible wrong. Do your schoolwork and be respectful, but commit in your heart and mind to studying God's Word and putting your faith in that alone.

I'm not going to tell you to believe the Bible without proof—I don't need to do that. There is plenty of proof and great explanations out there to show how science works with the scriptures to prove the Bible right. Believing in God's Word doesn't mean you have to deny scientific fact—they truly do fit together like a fascinating puzzle. It's very important that you do your studying and know why you believe what you do. Blind faith isn't necessarily wrong, but it sure won't help you share scriptural truths with others when they ask why you believe what you do.

Thy word have I hid in mine heart, that I might not sin against thee.
PSALM 119:11 KJV

63

A Child Shall Lead

Q: *My friend brought me to church a few times, and I liked it a lot! I got to know Jesus there. The problem is that now my parents will hardly ever let me go to church anymore because it's a different kind than they attended when they were kids. But they never even go to church now! My friend's church is really good, and they teach us the Bible very well, so there's nothing wrong with going there. Should I try to sneak and go to that church even though my parents said I couldn't?*

~Skylar

EMILY: No. You should never do something like that behind your parents' back. I'm sure they're trying to do what they think is right and aren't doing this to hurt you. Maybe you could invite them to go to church with you once and see what you're experiencing there. If they won't go, just pray about it and be patient. Something will work out.

NICOLE: Good idea, Em! I would start with that suggestion and invite them to go with you and check things out. Maybe it would be easier to get them to go if it's for something like a concert or play rather than an actual church service at first. If that doesn't work, you should definitely not go against their wishes by sneaking to the church. That would be a horrible Christian witness to them.

On the other hand, you do need to be in church so you can hear the Bible teachings and spend time with other Christians. So maybe for a while you'll need to find a place your parents approve of and start going there. You might have to go alone for a little while, but trust and pray that your parents will see their need to be there, too.

> *But thanks be to God! He gives us the victory through our Lord Jesus Christ.*
> 1 Corinthians 15:57 NIV

Choose Life

Q: *I hear a lot about abortion. Shouldn't abortion be okay if the mother is in danger? That makes sense to me, but I'm pretty sure Christians are supposed to believe that it's never okay to have an abortion.*

~Nina

NATALIE: I've had several people ask me what I think about that. It would sure be tough to face death in a risky pregnancy, or deal with a pregnancy in the case of a rape or something like that. But in reality, God never promised that life would be perfect, yet He calls us to trust Him. We have to trust that He'll work everything out just as He plans to and not do something wrong just because we're afraid or doubtful. I believe that abortion is wrong. It's taking the life of an innocent baby, and I can't think of any situation where I'd think that was okay to do, or that I'd want to do it.

NICOLE: Abortion is never the answer. Satan is logical and tugs at us where he can best affect us. A pregnant teen might feel hopeless, have regrets, wish things were different, etc., and Satan will capitalize on those feelings and try to get her to give up, think she has no choice or hope, and choose abortion.

It's important in those tough situations, even when facing grave danger, to trust that God is all-powerful and that He can work miracles. He never wants a person to sin (as abortion clearly is a sin) because of feeling hopeless—which is only a lack of trust in God.

Read the story of Shadrach, Meshach, and Abednego in Daniel 3. They allowed themselves to be thrown into a fiery furnace to be burned alive rather than sin against God. They knew He was capable of sparing them from certain death and trusted Him enough to face their fate even if He chose not to save them.

And my God will supply all your needs according to His riches in glory in Christ Jesus.
Philippians 4:19 nasb

Bruce Almighty

Q: *I often wonder if God actually has time to hear my prayers or know what's going on with me when so many people in the world are asking Him for help. How can I know for sure that He knows me and has time for me?*

~MARIAH

EMILY: If you prayed to Jesus and asked Him to be your Savior, then it's like He's your Father. Your heavenly Father always hears you, has time for you, listens to you, and answers your prayers. When I was a lot younger, I prayed to God all the time—like twice a week—for Him to forgive my sins and be my Savior. But I know now that I didn't need to pray that all the time. Once I asked Him into my life, He became my Father and I can trust that He hears me every time I call on Him.

NICOLE: Oh, I know! Isn't it amazing? It's like the president of the United States handing you a tissue when you sneeze. Or a superfamous singer coming to your birthday party just to sing "Happy Birthday" to you. Sometimes it even seems silly to pray about some of the things that seem important to us. With all He must see happen in the world, our concerns must be meaningless to God. Right? Oh, but that's so not the case.

The Bible says He knew you even before you were born and has every single hair on your head numbered. He knows when little birds fall to the ground—how much more does He pay attention to, care about, and want to be involved in every aspect of your life? Don't shut Him out just because you can't believe He wants in. He does!

> *"Whatever you ask in My name, that will I do, so that the Father may be glorified in the Son."*
> JOHN 14:13 NASB

66

Man vs. Ape

Q: *What do you do when your teacher is an evolutionist? Teachers pretty much laugh at the ideas held by Christians about the creation of the world. What can I do to really make them stop and think about what I believe?*

~TABITHA

NATALIE: Have you shared your testimony with your teacher? If you open your heart to her and to your class, maybe they would see that God is real to you and not just an idea from a textbook. Maybe you could write a letter outlining your beliefs with some scripture and other resources that support what you believe. In that letter, you could also ask that she not mock you or laugh at you in class.

NICOLE: Without getting into the argument about creation versus evolution, I can speak to the question of how to make them stop laughing at you and listen to your beliefs. The problem is, you can't really. You can't control how they respond to you any more than they can control your thinking. They believe they're right, and they're going to defend their position until something makes them sit up and take notice—usually the Holy Spirit nudging them in some way. You just need to continue being obedient by standing up for your beliefs and allow them to hold on to theirs if they choose to.

We're even told in the Bible that people will behave that way. Christians are encouraged in 2 Timothy to stay solid and teach truth no matter what.

Be ready to spread the word whether or not the time is right. Point out errors, warn people, and encourage them. Be very patient when you teach. A time will come when people will not listen to accurate teachings. Instead, they will follow their own desires and surround themselves with teachers who tell them what they want to hear. People will refuse to listen to the truth and turn to myths.
2 TIMOTHY 4:2–4 GW

Signs and Wonders

Q: *Has science disproved the miracles that Jesus performed? The creation of the universe, water into wine, the blind and lame healed, walking on the water. . . What does science say?*

~NICHOLE

NATALIE: One of the biggest things I hear about in science is the big bang theory and how we came about through the process of evolution. But the Bible talks about the seven days of creation when God made the heavens and the earth and everything in them. It specifically says in Genesis that God created man. I may not know enough about science to make a strong argument against evolution, but I choose to trust in God's Word because it has never steered me wrong before.

NICOLE: In order for scientists to prove or disprove something, they have to be able to re-create the event and test it. They observe the occurrences as they make it happen again and again, and then lay out their findings based on the observable fact. Since it's impossible for science to re-create the miracles of Christ, it would be foolish to look to science to determine if they're valid. Scientists are qualified to study natural things, but spiritual things are best left to the experts.

In questioning the validity of the miracles Jesus performed as recorded in scripture, one thing that stands out is the availability of eyewitness accounts. Many of the people who saw the miracles take place were still around when the words of scripture were written and didn't offer a single dispute to the stories. That's true for everything: the virgin birth, the resurrection of Lazarus, Jesus' resurrection, etc.

Eyewitness accounts, historical records, and the confirmation of faith are enough for me to believe in the miracles of God.

> *Jesus of Nazareth, a man approved of God unto you by mighty works and wonders and signs which God did by him in the midst of you, even as ye yourselves know. . .*
>
> ACTS 2:22 ASV

I'm So Mad!

Q: *Is it ever okay to be angry with God?*

~CAMRY

EMILY: I think it's probably best to fight against being angry with God, because we never really know the big picture of why He has allowed something to happen in our lives. It's probably natural to feel anger sometimes, and I don't think God would punish us for it, but I think it's best to pray about those feelings and ask God to forgive the anger.

NICOLE: Anger itself isn't a sin. It's a natural response to something that happened. God gets angry at us, and there are plenty of people in the Bible who were angry with God. People dealing with controlled anger were able to take their frustrations and disappointment to the Lord and express those feelings to Him in a way that He listened and responded. However, some of them were so consumed that they allowed their anger to grow into rage, which brought on God's wrath and punishment. That unbridled anger is sinful.

Again, it's not a sin to be angry with God. It becomes sin when you grip your feelings so tightly that they come between you and God. When that happens, it means that your feelings of self-righteousness have become more important to you than your relationship with Him. That blocks your faith and can lower your guard against other sin in your life.

When you're angry with God, you should first ask Him to show you why He allowed the pain in your life—whatever it is. Ask Him to forgive whatever part you had in it and to forgive your feelings toward Him. Then ask Him to help you forgive whoever might have wronged you.

Be angry and do not sin; do not let the sun go down on your anger.
EPHESIANS 4:26 ESV

69

For Such Is the Kingdom

Q: *I've always been taught that you have to confess that Jesus is Lord in order to be saved. You have to actually choose to serve Him, right? Well, my sister has a mental disability and can't understand that concept. Does that mean she won't go to heaven? I can't see how that would be fair—it's not her fault she can't grasp the concept of God's grace and her need for forgiveness. I can't imagine serving a God who would punish her for something she can't control. Can you help me figure this out?*

~SARAH

NATALIE: To be perfectly honest, I've struggled with this same topic. I can't really answer this because it would be fake for me to pretend I have an answer. I'm looking forward to learning from what Mom has to say on this.

NICOLE: Yeah, this is a common misunderstanding. It's very true that Jesus Christ is the only way to the Father, the only way to eternal salvation. If you are religious but don't know Christ, even if you give all your money to the poor or spend your life in service to God, He will say that He never knew you. This is non-negotiable and scripture is very, very clear on this.

However, when it comes to infants or the severely disabled, I don't believe this holds true because they cannot choose either way. They can't choose, nor can they reject. They haven't even been offered the opportunity to come to Christ. While that isn't an exception the Bible specifically makes, it's

only logical that it could be applied to people like your sister. Take a look at the verse below. Note that the people were bringing infants to Jesus and the disciples tried to keep them away.

> But Jesus called them to Him and said, "Let the little children come to Me, and do not forbid them; for of such is the kingdom of God. Assuredly, I say to you, whoever does not receive the kingdom of God as a little child will by no means enter it."
> LUKE 18:16–17 NKJV

Be Still and Listen

Q: *How do I know what God's will is? How do I know if I'm called to ministry?*
                                              ~Danae

NATALIE: You might not always know exactly what God's ultimate will is for the rest of your life in detail, but you can follow His leading for the next step you're to take. You don't have to have all of the answers up front—in fact, sometimes He works like that to help us learn to trust Him. If we move ahead when He leads us, then we can say it was all Him.

NICOLE: We're all called to be ministers of God's love to others. I know what you're asking, though. You want to know how to know if God is calling you to be a missionary to Africa or a writer, singer, teacher, etc. God's calling is going to come from within your passions and talents. It's going to be so strong that you won't be happy until you do whatever it is you feel called to do.

Take teaching for example. That can definitely be a calling from God whether it's lived out in a church or school setting. Public, secular employment can be God's calling just as much as missions work. People think ministries like missions, speaking, preaching, singing, writing, etc., are more glamorous or important to God than what others might call regular jobs. The key is to live as a minister called by God to reach people with His love—wherever you're planted.

God made you just the way you are with your own special talents and desires. Take a look at yourself and consider those clues into what God might have for you to do, and then commit to serving Him in anything and everything you do.

> *"Ask and it will be given to you; seek and you will find; knock and the door will be opened to you."*
> Matthew 7:7 niv

Why?

Q: *Why does God allow bad things to happen? If He has the power to make everything better and to heal people from terrible illness and to prevent accidents, why doesn't He?*

~CHEYENNE

EMILY: Oh wow. This is a really hard one. I think Christians just trust that God has everything in control and that He knows the reasons why things happen the way they do. I wish I had a better answer, though—truth is, I'm as confused by this as you are. I do have faith in God and trust Him with my life, my future, and my family.

NICOLE: Okay, girls. I hear the confusion. . .and I get it. Let's take a look at what God has to say about this question. The book of Isaiah is amazing. Truly, it contains everything you'd need to know about God—past, present, future. If you didn't have any of the rest of the Bible, you could figure out what God did in the past, who Jesus is and what He did for you, and what your future holds in the kingdom of God. Amazing truths! Isaiah 55 assures us that God has a plan and that His ways are not the same as our ways.

God doesn't want us to endure hardship. In fact, He wanted this earth to be a perfect reflection of His Kingdom. But sin took hold and we've been fighting against the flesh ever since. In our earthly bodies, we're to fight the good fight of faith, make it through the sin and evil of this world, and suffer the things that come against us in this world. One day, when we stand before God, faithfully having endured all we faced in our earthly lives, we will hear the words, "Well done, my good and faithful servant."

> *But when Jesus heard it he said, "This illness does not lead to death. It is for the glory of God, so that the Son of God may be glorified through it."*
> JOHN 11:4 ESV

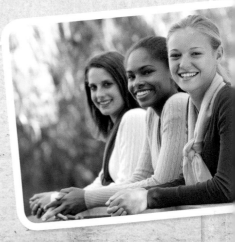

Words of Life

Q: *My Sunday school class was talking about curse words the other day. I get that it's bad to take God's name in vain. But my Sunday school teacher said it's bad to say "OMG" and stuff like that. She even said that we should stop and think about words like "gosh," "goodness," and "geez" because they stand for "God." What do you think?*

~P.J.

EMILY: I don't really get the whole swearing thing, anyway. Why do people feel the need to talk like that in the first place? I mean, if there's any question about what you're saying, why not just pick something else to say?

I don't know for sure if words like "gosh" and saying "OMG" are wrong, but my mom asks me not to say them because they just aren't necessary and it's better not to do something if you aren't sure. In the end, though, I think you have to look at what you mean by the words—that's the most important thing.

NICOLE: There is some debate in Christian circles over whether or not it's okay to use some of those words. I think the best thing to do is to examine your heart when you say them. What are you meaning by them? Also, what might other people feel by your expression? You never want to say something that might damage your witness or cause someone else to stumble.

I definitely want to encourage you to obey your parents when it comes to your language and to take careful notice of what your church teaches. Worse than actually saying the words would be to go against the wishes of the people God has put in authority over you.

A favorite old quote says that you are what you do when no one is looking. So, if you're disobeying your parents just because they aren't around, it is a true reflection of the condition of your heart toward them and toward God.

> *Don't use foul or abusive language. Let everything you say be good and helpful, so that your words will be an encouragement to those who hear them.*
> EPHESIANS 4:29 NLT

True Love

Q: *What is true love, and how do you know when you have found it? As followers of Christ, we can only identify true love when we have found it based on what the Word of God says. So what does the Bible say about "true love"?*

~Danielle

NATALIE: I was just reading my Bible today and came across 1 Corinthians 13:4–5, which says that love is patient and kind. It isn't jealous or prideful. It doesn't dishonor people—like gossip, teasing, slander. It isn't self-seeking, meaning it puts others first. Love doesn't jump to anger or get upset easily. It keeps no record of wrongs; it lets go of the past without throwing it up in your face all the time. If you can substitute the pronoun "it" with the name of the person you're dating, then you might be close.

In loving someone else, you need to see him through God's eyes. Recognize the potential that God has for him, and allow him to be imperfect as long as he's striving for God's best.

NICOLE: I really don't have a lot to add to that answer, Natalie. I want to focus on the aspect of being lovable rather than searching for love. Boys you might take an interest in right now are on the same path to being shaped by God's refining fire as you are. They aren't ready to be held to love's standards, and neither are you.

Pray that God will continue to mold and shape you so that you're ready one day when the time comes for you to find love. Also, pray for your husband—he's out there somewhere, so pray that God will be working in his life.

Love does not delight in evil but rejoices with the truth. It always protects, always trusts, always hopes, always perseveres.
1 Corinthians 13:6–7 niv

Relationship

Q: *What does having a relationship with God really mean?*

~TARYN

EMILY: It means that you follow God's Word and make it a part of your everyday life. You trust Jesus with your life and let Him guide you. You look to Him for help and guidance and kind of hang with Him on a daily basis. Basically, it's like He's your best friend.

NICOLE: Yes. The word *relationship* implies an ongoing connection. It's more than choosing a religion. It's more than accepting Jesus as your personal Savior. Having a relationship with God means you walk with Him. It means you pray and communicate with God about decisions you have to make and needs you might have. It means you study His Word and strive to know Him—I mean *really* know Him. All of that takes work.

"Here I am! I stand at the door and knock. If anyone hears my voice and opens the door, I will come in and eat with that person, and they with me."
REVELATION 3:20 NIV

Relationship is an ongoing process that never completely arrives at a conclusion. It's a living, breathing entity that exists between you and God and is personal only to you. You can get as much out of it as you want to put into it. Funny enough, human relationships work the same way, don't they?

Cultivating your relationship with God is the best thing you can do, and you should start now by purposing to know Him more and to make Him part of every moment of your life.

Tolerance: The Unloving Choice

Q: *I'm confused. I thought that Christians were supposed to stand strong and not back down from our beliefs when people try to water them down or deny them as fact. But these days, all you hear about is tolerance. Tolerating everyone's different beliefs might be politically correct, but is that what God wants from followers of Christ?*

~LILA

NATALIE: In some situations it's great to be tolerant of others, but allowing people to believe things that could hurt them or keep them from God isn't a loving choice. In a way, you're keeping them from the type of relationship with God that you have by not pointing them to the truth and then defending it.

NICOLE: I heard a story once about a woman who accepted Christ after her children were in high school. She had a radical conversion and became a real evangelist, spreading the message of Christ to everyone she knew. Over time, she began to get a little frustrated as she thought back to all of the kids in her own high school who were part of the local youth groups. Why had none of them reached out to her? Why had none of them shared their faith with her? Being the natural evangelist she was, how many more people might have come to know the Lord if she'd had those twenty years to serve God? Plus, her kids would have had a much different childhood if they'd been raised in church and taught about the Lord from an early age.

The problem is that too many people are tolerant of all beliefs and they don't want to take a stand for anything anymore. There are some things about God and the Bible that aren't salvation dependent and shouldn't become a basis for arguments and division. But some of it—like who Jesus is and how a person can be saved—those things are battles you need to fight with complete intolerance of other teachings.

But don't mistake intolerance with hate. Standing firm on the truth of the Word of God is the most loving thing you can do for unbelievers.

> *For the word of God is alive and active. Sharper than any double-edged sword, it penetrates even to dividing soul and spirit, joints and marrow; it judges the thoughts and attitudes of the heart.*
> HEBREWS 4:12 NIV

Road Map

Q: *What does God expect of me? How am I supposed to live, and how do I know what I'm supposed to do with my life?*

~LILLIANA

EMILY: God expects you to do what's right and follow His will. Living according to the guidelines in the Bible will lead you to His will. The Word of God is the road map to your future.

NICOLE: Those are huge questions! You'd think they'd need a huge answer, right?

Wrong.

How are you supposed to live, and how do you know what you're supposed to do with your life? The answer is really simple: *ask Him.*

I know that sounds oversimplified, but it's really the only way. You can learn about God's will by reading His Word and praying for guidance in how you can apply it to your daily life. You can grow to know Jesus by having an ongoing, daily relationship with Him, communicating with Him about your worries and fears, and trusting in His promises. You can pray and ask specifically for guidance as you take steps and make decisions.

Isaiah 30:21 promises that you'll hear Him, that a voice behind you will point the way to go, whether to the right or the left. Ask that He close doors if something you want for your future is not part of His plan for your life. Conversely, ask that He open doors to show you the direction He wants you to go; believe that He'll reveal to you exactly what you need to know, when you need to know it. Ultimately, just walk with Him. Make Him a living, breathing, vibrant part of your life, and ask Him.

> *Trust in the LORD with all your heart; do not depend on your own understanding. Seek his will in all you do, and he will show you which path to take.*
> PROVERBS 3:5–6 NLT

Simple Assurance

Q: *My uncle was a Christian, but he committed suicide about a month ago. Someone from my school said he can't get into heaven. Is that true? And how can I help my family through this?*

~BREE

NATALIE: Salvation comes as a free gift from God. I don't believe that suicide would keep a person who already knew God from entering heaven. We've all sinned, and suicide is no different than any other sin. God doesn't break His promises, so I believe you'll see your uncle again one day. The best way to help your family is to show them how much God loves your uncle and how much He loves them.

NICOLE: Bree, I'm so very sorry for your loss. This must be a very difficult time for your family. Natalie's answer actually reminded me of one of my favorite verses, which is a promise from God. We're told in Philippians that God started the work in all believers—that He called them to Himself and will be faithful to complete that work when they see Jesus.

How does that apply to your uncle? It's a simple assurance that God has been faithful and completed the work in your uncle. His earthly actions in no way detract from the grace of God or destroy the power of the blood of Christ that covers our sin. Your uncle received that grace when he accepted Jesus Christ as his Lord.

You see, God made salvation dependent on nothing but the blood of Christ. If it were based on what we do or don't do, then we wouldn't have needed a Savior. We'd have to fight our whole lives to earn our way into heaven. Thankfully, once we receive that free gift of grace, the Father sees us through the blood of His Son.

> *"I can guarantee this truth: People will be forgiven for any sin or curse."*
> MARK 3:28 GW

Color Blind

Q: *Is interracial marriage biblical? Is it godly for a white man to marry a black woman and vice versa? What does the Bible teach about this controversial topic?*

~Blair

NATALIE: I don't know exactly what the Bible says about it, but I can't imagine that it would be wrong. God created us all in His image, and our skin color doesn't matter to Him, so it shouldn't matter to us. I think the way the world is, mixed marriages like that can create some struggles—but that has nothing to do what God thinks. It's just because people are dumb and prejudiced.

NICOLE: Wow, Natster. That's a great answer, and you're absolutely right. Blair, interracial marriage isn't wrong according to God in any way. In fact, He would prefer that people didn't see color—the only reason He sees it is to appreciate the beauty in His creation, not to create division.

Natalie is right, though. In this world, there are a lot of hardships that come with doing anything outside the box. People are judgmental and full of all sorts of prejudice. Those types of people can give mixed-race couples and families a pretty hard time. That's in no way saying people shouldn't marry outside their race; it just means that they need to be aware of the hardships that come with it.

> *As a result, there is no longer any distinction between Gentiles and Jews, circumcised and uncircumcised, barbarians, savages, slaves, and free, but Christ is all, Christ is in all.*
> Colossians 3:11 GNT

Cast the First Stone

Q: *There are openly gay students in my high school—like dating each other. As a Christian, how should I treat them when I believe that what they do is wrong?*
~FAITH

NATALIE: I don't think you should ever treat people any differently just because you believe that what they're doing is wrong. Everyone makes mistakes and sins—and it's not up to us to decide whether or not they deserve our judgment. Would you feel this way if a boy and a girl were having sex? What's the difference, in God's eyes? It's a sexual relationship outside of marriage. Your job, as a Christian, is to be Jesus to the people you interact with every day. This means loving them, not judging them.

NICOLE: Great point, Natalie! I'm reminded of the story of the woman caught in adultery. She was brought before Jesus to be punished for her crime. In those days, the penalty was a public stoning. Jesus asked her accusers to examine themselves. Whoever among them could find no sin in his heart could go ahead and throw the first stone. They all left. No one accused her because they were all guilty of something themselves.

Just like Natalie said, there are other students at your school engaging in premarital sex. Some are doing drugs. Some are drinking alcohol and driving a car. Do you see? No sin is any different in God's eyes. The way you should treat these teens, and everyone, is the way Jesus treated the woman caught in adultery—with love, compassion, and kindness. However, He didn't pretend the sin was okay. He told her she was forgiven but then instructed that she go and sin no more. In the same way, you can be an example to these friends and uphold God's Word so that when the time comes, you're a credible witness of His will.

> *The majority of you have imposed a severe enough punishment on that person. So now forgive and comfort him. Such distress could overwhelm someone like that if he's not forgiven and comforted. That is why I urge you to assure him that you love him.*
> 2 CORINTHIANS 2:6–8 GW

Power to Heal

Q: *What should a Christian do if she is overwhelmed with depression? Is it right to use antidepressant drugs? Or should a Christian's faith be enough to solve depression problems?*

~CHRISTA

NATALIE: I don't have a lot of insight into this one because I don't know much about it. I do know that God can heal anything, but I also know that He gave doctors and chemists brains to come up with treatments for illnesses, too. Depression is a real problem, so I don't think it would be fair to just throw out the possibility of using medication to treat it.

NICOLE: Great question! Depression is an illness. It can be caused by an event or by a chemical process in the body. It's real and it's not something to play around with. Mild depression might go away in time, or with counseling, prayer, diversion, etc. But serious depression can cause all sorts of problems in relationships, and can even have serious risks like self-injury, suicide, or abuse.

If my daughter were suffering from depression, I would take the following steps:

- Pray for wisdom.
- Talk to her as openly and often as possible.
- Pray for wisdom.
- Seek counseling for her and maybe for me to know how to help her.
- Pray for wisdom.
- See a medical doctor about medication if necessary.
- Pray for wisdom.

Do you see? There's not one pat answer or perfect course of action. I wouldn't want to make this decision on my own, so I would seek the help of medical professionals along with guidance from the Lord. But no, I don't think antidepressants are wrong when they are needed. They are medications just like cancer drugs and antibiotics. I do think they can be misused or overused, which is why prayer and guidance from God are so important.

I prayed to the LORD,
and he answered me.
He freed me from all my fears.
PSALM 34:4 NLT

Right Is Right, Right? Right!

Q: *Is right and wrong a definite black-and-white thing anymore? It seems like people change their thoughts on what's okay based on what they want to do. So how do we know for sure? I mean, is there a way to really decide with complete certainty if something is okay with God?*

~COLLETTE

EMILY: The only way to know for sure if something is okay with God is to see if it matches up with His will. You can pray to Him, read the Bible, and ask yourself if it's something Jesus would do. If it doesn't match up with scripture, or you think it's not something Jesus would do, then you pretty much have your answer.

NICOLE: Yes. Right and wrong. Black and white. Sin is still absolute. Times may have changed, but God hasn't. In fact, the increase in communication ability, technology, media, etc., has just made it easier to sin and provided more opportunities for it. Just because it's easier doesn't mean we should lower our standards—or that God has lowered His.

Back in Bible times and throughout history, and in many places in the world still today, people have lost their lives for their faith. They stand on the Word of God and don't compromise even to the point of death.

What are we talking about here? A little peer pressure? Some temptations to do enticing things? God hasn't compromised—and He won't.

Jesus Christ never changes! He is the same yesterday, today, and forever.
HEBREWS 13:8 CEV

It's Not about You

Q: *If God forgives me every time I ask, why do I still feel so guilty? If God forgives these sins and doesn't even remember them, why doesn't the guilt go away?*

~Petra

NATALIE: It's natural to feel regret for the things you've done. You still have to deal with the consequences of what you've done. It might have lasting effects on your reputation or your relationships. Even though God has forgiven you, you need to learn to forgive yourself. It can be a long process, and even when you think you've done it, the guilt might creep back in. Just turn your guilt into thankfulness for what God has done for you.

NICOLE: Guilt isn't from God. Guilt and regret are tools of the enemy to keep you mired in the past and to remind you of what you've done. Satan doesn't want to let you move on from it to walk in the fullness of God's grace, because that would mean he had no power over you any longer.

You need to do a little bit of studying about the grace of God and forgiveness. He has offered you this free gift, and it sounds like you accept it but then give it right back because of your own guilt and doubt. You're trusting too much in yourself and in how worthy you are for salvation and forgiveness. You're missing the mark. It's not about you; it's about *Him*. He is worthy. His blood is sufficient. His grace makes you whole. You can't make yourself good enough, so free your soul of the weight of guilt and receive freedom from the penalty of sin through the mercy of Christ.

And their sins and their iniquities will I remember no more.
Hebrews 10:17 ASV

83

Check It Out

Q: *What do I do if a friend invites me to her church, but it's not the same kind of church I go to? How do I know when to stand up, when to sit down, etc.? I don't want to look like someone who doesn't go to church. And is it even okay to go to a church that's different than mine?*

~LIZ

EMILY: It really depends on the different kind of church. If they teach things about the Bible that aren't true or don't teach the Bible, then you should probably stick with your own church. If it's just a matter of different styles, but the church still has good Bible teaching, then it's perfectly fine to go check it out.

NICOLE: Interesting question, Liz. Honestly, I wouldn't worry about it. You can follow the cues of the people around you or talk to your friend ahead of time. Or, if you're really concerned and want to do some study ahead of time, you could Google the denomination (type of church) and see what it says about the church services.

Whatever you decide, Jesus died for your sins, rose from the dead, and is on the throne at the right hand of the Father. His grace is all you need to cover your sins, and you'll spend eternity with Him. Those truths right there, they're all that matters. It doesn't matter if people stand up, sit down, turn around. . .put their right foot in. . .shake it all about (okay, I got carried away!). But you know what I'm saying, I'm sure. It's about the truth, not about the style. Enjoy learning and experiencing the way different people worship—there's beauty in all sorts of styles.

The most important thing, again, is the truth. You don't want to visit a church that says anything different about Jesus than what I said above. There are not many ways to heaven. We don't pray to the universe or a higher power. It's not okay to tolerate teachings that say those things. So check out the church, but make sure you know what you believe first.

> *In the same way, even though we are many individuals, Christ makes us one body and individuals who are connected to each other.*
> ROMANS 12:5 GW

Good Enough

Q: *How do I know if I'm good enough to go to heaven? I'm a good person. I try to help people when I can. I try not to lie or gossip—even though I mess up sometimes. I seriously doubt I'll ever do anything really wrong like murder or something. Is that enough?*

~ABIGAIL

NATALIE: It's not about being good enough, doing enough, living well enough. . .enough, enough. You are saved by asking God to forgive your sins and accepting Jesus as your Lord. Really. That's it. You move on from there and try to do God's will and live a life pleasing to Him. But that's part of the growth process—not part of the salvation process.

> *God saved you through faith as an act of kindness. You had nothing to do with it. Being saved is a gift from God. It's not the result of anything you've done, so no one can brag about it.*
> EPHESIANS 2:8–9 GW

NICOLE: Right, Nat. There's a difference between salvation and relationship. Salvation is what happens at the moment you enter a relationship with God. Think of it like a pregnancy—the moment a baby is conceived, that human being is forever the child of his parents. The same is true with salvation and your heavenly Father. That's how you get to heaven—that moment of conception.

Following the time a baby is conceived, every minute for the rest of his life is an opportunity for relationship building. He can choose to invest whatever amount of time, and show a lot of respect and obedience to his parents.

Irrelevant

Q: *Some of the things the Bible says are so old-fashioned and out of touch with real life today. Don't we need to soften our approach to right and wrong, or change the expectations we put on ourselves and others, in order to stay relevant to the issues people actually face today?*

~Phoebe

NATALIE: I totally get what you're saying about the Bible seeming out of touch. I love to use Bible study books directed toward teens to help me wade through the issues because they make it seem more real and personal to my own life. I even like to read Christian fiction because it helps me to see God in today's society and kind of put myself in the positions people face and see how they might handle things.

Even though it seems tough sometimes, I do believe the Bible is relevant to us today, and I don't think we should change the way we read it or apply it to our lives.

NICOLE: Yeah, that's an old argument that people use to make excuses for why they can't—or don't—stand up to sin. God is still God. He is the same yesterday, today, and forever. Nothing that happens today was off His radar grid when He handed down His Word. You'd be surprised if you really dug into the Bible and saw what kinds of relevant things are covered.

In fact, I'd say the expectations should be higher for Christians today because we have so much help and so many Bible-based resources right at our fingertips. Instead of following God's will just because He said so, we're able to flesh out the whys and hows of scripture, get counseling when we need it, and worship with believers on a weekly basis or more.

The cool part is that the grace of God covers contemporary, modern problems as much as it did the ancient ones. God's will hasn't changed pertaining to sin and His expectations of believers, but it also hasn't changed in regard to His love and mercy. Perfect!

Jesus Christ is the same yesterday, today, and forever.
Hebrews 13:8 GW

Find the Truth

Q: *Aren't all religions basically the same? According to a poll, many Americans assume that when Christians, Jews, Buddhists, and others pray to their god, they're all actually praying to the same god, just using different names for that deity.*

~ROBIN

EMILY: I've wondered about this for a while, but I believe that the only way to be saved and go to heaven is to pray to Jesus and ask Him to forgive your sins. There's no other way to find forgiveness, so I'd have to say that the only way to know if a god is really God is to find out what other religions teach about Jesus.

NICOLE: No. God is very, very clear that the only way to get to Him—the one, true God—is through His Son, Jesus Christ. You'd have to take a look at each of those faiths and find out what they think about Jesus. Here's what you need to ask:

- Did Jesus walk on earth?
- Is He the Son of God?
- Did He die on a cross?
- Was He resurrected from the dead?
- Is He the only way to salvation?

Answering no to any of those questions tells you beyond a shadow of a doubt that the religion is not serving the true God. He isn't interested in worship that overlooks the sacrifice of Christ. The blood of Jesus is the only payment for sin that He will accept.

Many faiths believe that final sacrifice is yet to come—that Jesus wasn't it. But Christians know differently. Don't make the mistake of watering down your faith by opening yourself up to the lie that all faiths are the same.

"And there is salvation in no one else, for there is no other name under heaven given among men by which we must be saved."
ACTS 4:12 ESV

Jesus said to him, "I am the way, and the truth, and the life. No one comes to the Father except through me."
JOHN 14:6 ESV

Prayer and Fasting

Q: *What does it mean to fast? Should teenagers do it?*

~Holly

EMILY: Fasting is like praying with sacrifice. We just learned that the other day. I've never done it yet, but I think it's a great idea. It's like saying, "I'm willing to give this up, because this other thing is so important to me."

NICOLE: Yeah, that pretty much is what fasting is, Em. But Holly, it goes a bit deeper than that, too. The point of fasting isn't just to sacrifice something; it's also to replace it with something else. So if your fast is food related, then you're going to take the time, energy, and focus you put into food preparation and consumption, and give it back to God in prayer. The same principle applies to watching television, reading, surfing the Web. It's a replacement as well as a sacrifice.

Don't make the mistake of treating your fast as a sort of spiritual blackmail. You're not trying to force God's hand like people used to do with hunger strikes. Nor are you trying to make a bargain: "I gave this up for You; now You give me this." It definitely doesn't work that way.

Should you fast? Well, it depends on your motivations. If you examine your heart and find that your ultimate desire is to draw closer to God and hear His voice, then sure, it's a beautiful thing. Decide in advance exactly what it is you're going to fast, and for how long. Then determine to commit to it, and replace it with prayer and focus on God.

> *"When you fast, stop looking sad like hypocrites. They put on sad faces to make it obvious that they're fasting. I can guarantee this truth: That will be their only reward."*
> MATTHEW 6:16 GW

Change of Heart

Q: *I'm in a gang. Can God save me even if I can't get out of the gang? What if I do drugs and other stuff like that? Sometimes I feel like there's no point in even trying to be good enough. It's just not going to happen where I'm from.*

~Maria

NATALIE: Of course God can save you. He is powerful enough to forgive you for your sins and to pull you from your circumstances. He may not choose to get you out of them, though. Instead, He may want to use you for His purposes in the midst of where you are. No matter what, trust in His power and wisdom. He'll get you through whatever happens when you turn from sin and turn toward Him.

NICOLE: Let's take a look at some people in the Bible who were saved from horrible things—even worse than gangs. Saul was one of the chief persecutors of Christians. He slaughtered people because of their faith in God. One day on the road to Damascus, he had a supernatural encounter with Jesus and made a dynamic conversion. He immediately turned from his old life and began to preach the Word (Acts 9). Another example is the woman caught in adultery (John 8). Jesus forgave her for her sin, then told her to go and sin no more.

You see, forgiveness is available to everyone, for everything. However, true repentance means to turn from the behavior. If you're sorry for something and continue to do it, it may mean you weren't really interested in forgiveness as much as afraid of consequences. Realize that everyone faces the temptation to sin and take the easy way through this world, but God promises to always give you a way out from under that stronghold if you'll accept it.

I'm not going to tell you that you can't be forgiven every time you mess up—you can. That forgiveness is there for you. But a true conversion will be declared by a changed heart that will not tolerate a life of sin any longer.

> *"And I will give you a new heart, and a new spirit I will put within you. And I will remove the heart of stone from your flesh and give you a heart of flesh."*
> EZEKIEL 36:26 ESV

The Lamb of God

Q: *I read in the Bible about how people killed lambs and other animals to pay for their own sins. Why don't we still do that? And if we don't, are we going to be able to have our sins forgiven?*

~SKYLAR

NATALIE: We don't do that anymore because that was before Jesus was even born. Before Christ, people had no other way to pay for their sins. Now we have the blood of Christ, the true Lamb, who died on the cross to pay for our sins. We don't need to sacrifice animals because we have the Lamb of God as the final sacrifice.

NICOLE: Blood has always been required by God to pay the price for sins. In the Old Testament, people had to atone for their sins by sacrificing a spotless, blemish-free animal, and that blood requirement to cover sins was met in that way. Human beings are incapable of atoning for (paying for) their sins—not by being good enough, nor by sacrifice. We can't ever make good on our debt.

That's why Jesus came and presented Himself as that perfect, spotless, sin-less Lamb who would pay the price for sins, once and for all. His death was the final atonement sacrifice and it is sufficient to pay for all of our sins—past, present, and future. That's what He meant when He cried from the cross, "It is finished."

The next day he saw Jesus coming toward him, and said, "Behold, the Lamb of God, who takes away the sin of the world!"
JOHN 1:29 ESV

By sending his own Son in the likeness of sinful flesh and for sin, he condemned sin in the flesh, in order that the righteous requirement of the law might be fulfilled in us, who walk not according to the flesh but according to the Spirit.
ROMANS 8:3–4 ESV

Jesus Saves

Q: *How can I know Jesus personally?*

~MELISSA

EMILY: On Sunday mornings when I go to church, I enjoy the worship time the most. It helps me feel really close to God and kind of leads me into prayer.

NATALIE: The way I know Jesus personally is that I have quiet time with my Bible and various study books. By studying about Him, I learn about His character and my relationship with Him grows. I also love my youth group because it helps me relate to God on my own level. I always feel closer to God after I'm with other believers my own age.

NICOLE: The first step in knowing Jesus personally is admitting that you have sinned (Romans 3:23) and that sin must be paid for (Romans 6:23). Once you realize that you're unable to take care of that sin on your own, you find that Jesus did it for you (Romans 5:8). If you believe that Jesus did what you couldn't do, and you profess your faith in Him, you're saved (Romans 10:9–13).

That's a quick rundown of the basics of salvation. Moving on from that moment of faith and forgiveness, you become washed in the grace and mercy of God, who no longer sees you in your sin, but sees you through the blood of His Son. You are then at peace and in relationship with Jesus Christ (Romans 5:1).

Have you made that step and reached toward the forgiveness you can only find through Jesus? If you have not, but are ready to now, simply pray the following prayer:

> *Lord, I know I'm a sinner and I deserve to be punished. I believe that Jesus took my punishment on Himself and offers me forgiveness. I want to walk in that grace and mercy and receive it right now. I trust in You. Thank You for Your grace and forgiveness, and for eternal life. Amen!*

> *For I am convinced that neither death nor life, neither angels nor demons, neither the present nor the future, nor any powers, neither height nor depth, nor anything else in all creation, will be able to separate us from the love of God that is in Christ Jesus our Lord.*
> ROMANS 8:38–39 NIV

THE "FAM"

Christmas Cheer

Q: *I'm having a hard time this Christmas because my parents just got divorced. I have to be at my dad's house when my mom and aunts and uncles are at my grandma's house opening presents. I want to be at both places, but I can't. I just feel like I'd rather not go anywhere and just sit in my room instead. It's like they got divorced and now I have to suffer. I asked them to change their schedule so I could be at both places, but they won't. What should I do?*

~ASHLEY

EMILY: It's a tough thing to have to deal with—believe me, I know. This happens to me sometimes even though my parents do their best to make sure I can be at every event. My advice is to just try to make the best of it. Focus on making your own party wherever you go. Then when you're the grown-up, you can set your own traditions. Plus, things have a way of working out. Things seem to change all the time, and what was a problem this year won't be next year. Just go with it. It'll make it better for you and for everyone.

NICOLE: Hi, Ashley. I'm so sorry for what you're going through. I think parents don't always understand how difficult this situation is for the kids, but I can promise that yours don't mean to make it rough on you. I know it's hard; nothing I can say will change that fact. But like Emily said, *you* are in complete control of your mood, your attitude, and your own fun. Your parents love you, you'll have time with both of them, you'll get to celebrate Christmas twice. . .enjoy whatever it is instead of wishing for what it isn't.

> *"I will never leave you nor forsake you."*
> HEBREWS 13:5 ESV

God Makes No Mistakes

Q: *My brother, Ben, is the sweetest boy on earth. His favorite thing to give or receive is a hug—from anyone. In case you haven't guessed, Ben has Down syndrome. This is a disorder that makes him look and act different than other people. In many ways, he's much better than other people. He'd never hurt someone. He'd never be dishonest. He'd never take something that didn't belong to him. But in other ways his differences make him stand out and get picked on. People just don't understand how good he is; they just pick on his weaknesses. I try to spread the word and protect him when I can, but I can't be there all the time. And sometimes when he tries to hug my friends, I get embarrassed. What should I do?*

~ALLIE

EMILY: If your mom doesn't know that Ben is getting picked on, you should talk to her about it and try to come up with a solution to avoid those situations. I also think you should talk to your friends ahead of time and let them know that Ben might hug them, and explain why he does it. You might find out they don't mind at all. Above all, keep doing your best to protect him—he needs you.

NICOLE: What a wonderful big sister! It's so great that your brother has someone like you to look out for him. I understand how difficult it is to feel different, though. You didn't mention how old you and your brother are, so I can't be specific to your ages, but it's clear you feel protective, like a big sister.

Don't let people's reactions to your brother bother you; just let those actions and responses to Ben show you what's really inside people's hearts. You can learn a lot about them by the way they respond to your brother's eager friendship. Protecting Ben from hurtful people is more important than hanging out with the cool kids. I'm sure you already knew that, though.

> *Friends always show their love.*
> *What are relatives for if*
> *not to share trouble?*
> PROVERBS 17:17 GNT

Pamper Mom

Q: *This question is mainly for Nicole. I'd like to do something really special for my mom since she works so hard and has been a single mom for a long time. She loves me and my brother and never yells at us. I know she's tired and wishes things could be different. How can I let her know that I love her in a special way without any money?*

~MELANY

NICOLE: I'm so glad you wrote. I think it's so wonderful—and too rare—that you can recognize your mom's hard work and dedication. Single moms have it really rough because they have to bring in money to support the household plus care for you kids and hopefully have some fun with you, too.

It would be my guess that your mom doesn't get much time to pamper herself. What if you gave her a spa day? Wake her up with breakfast in bed. It doesn't have to be elaborate, even a bowl of cereal and a cup of coffee would be enjoyable. Tell her the day is all for her to relax. No work. You can give her a manicure: massage her hands with lotion, file her nails, paint them a pretty color. Let her soak her feet in a warm pan of salt water. Maybe even let her take a hot bubble bath and then give her a shoulder massage. These are all things you can do to make her feel really special without having to spend a dime.

While she's soaking in the bath, you could take it one step further by straightening up the house, preparing something for lunch, etc. You get the idea.

The key is, it's not about buying her something or completely changing her life. You just want to show her that you notice all she does, you love her and appreciate her, and you care about how she feels.

"Every one of you shall reverence his mother."
LEVITICUS 19:3 NASB

Military Dad

Q: *My dad's in the military, and he is gone a lot. He's in Afghanistan right now. I'm proud of him, but I miss him a lot, and Mom and I aren't getting along very well. What can I do?*

~Chloe

EMILY: It must be really hard to be away from your dad, but I can definitely understand why you're proud of him! It's important to keep him a part of your daily life as best you can, so you should write him letters and talk on the phone with him as much as possible. You and your mom need to pull together more than ever while your dad is away. Try to do some things together and be open with her about how you feel. You're both under a lot of stress and seem to be taking it out on each other. If you talk about it, you might be better able to face it together.

NICOLE: Well, you're very right to be proud of your dad. It has to be very difficult to be so far away from your loved ones and to sacrifice so much. I, for one, am so very grateful for him and for others like him who are willing to serve and defend our country.

I'm very sorry you and your mom aren't getting along right now. You have a couple of things going against you. First of all, the normal mother/teen conflict that is usually brought on by hormone fluctuations and natural changes that take place as a girl becomes a woman. Some of that is normal and would be happening whether your dad were home or not. Secondly, your mom has the added strain of living as a single mom right now. Cut her some slack if you can. She's likely doing her best to keep everything flowing in your dad's absence. It's a very difficult thing to do. Finally, you both have to deal with missing your dad. It's hard to have him so far away, so maybe you two could pull together and support each other in that rather than fight against each other.

> *Casting all your care upon him; for he careth for you.*
> 1 PETER 5:7 KJV

The Big Picture

Q: *I want to know my family history, but my dad doesn't like to talk about his family or his childhood because he has bad memories. I'm an only child, as was my dad, so if I don't get the information from him, it'll be lost forever. What should I do?*

~Tracee

EMILY: You're kind of making me wonder about my own family history. I haven't ever really gotten into that, but you bring up a really good point. In your case, I think the information is important, but I don't think you should put your dad through any kind of pain so you can get the info you want. In the big picture, it's just knowledge about the past. Your dad's feelings and hurts are real and current.

NICOLE: Emily made some excellent points, Tracee. There's no way for you to really know how difficult it is for your dad to let his mind travel back to those memories and those people. I wouldn't recommend that you badger him about it. I don't think there's anything wrong with bringing it up once in a while and letting him know that whenever, if ever, he's ready to talk about it, you're ready. The important thing is to not make your dad feel like he's letting you down. He needs to work through his past before he can open it up to you. Feeling pressured to do that might make him close up even tighter.

It might get easier for your dad over time. If not, worse things will happen in life than losing track of your family history. If it's super important to you, there are organizations that will trace your genealogy for you, but wait until you have your dad's permission or you're an adult. When the time is right, definitely pursue the research and keep careful records. You never know when that information might come in handy.

But our citizenship is in heaven. And we eagerly await a Savior from there, the Lord Jesus Christ.
Philippians 3:20 niv

99

The New Girl

Q: *Everything was going great. I was doing awesome in school. I'd made the cheerleading squad, and I had lots of friends. Then my parents got divorced. I had to move away and everything changed. Why did my parents have to get divorced and ruin my life?*

~Kat

EMILY: I'm so sorry that happened. Divorce is never easy, but I guarantee your parents didn't get divorced to ruin your life. The choice they made was so that you'd all have a better life. Whether you agree with that or can see how it's true, it almost certainly was their reason. You can't see the whole picture, but in your parents' minds, the pain of the divorce was less than the pain that staying together would have caused. It's just really hard to accept that when you had no say in the decision.

My parents are also divorced. It wasn't easy and it still isn't, but I've found that a lot of good came out of a tough situation.

NICOLE: Oh, I'm so sorry for all you've been through, Kat. Divorce is hard on everyone—trust us, we know all about that in this family. One thing I can say with 100 percent certainty is that your parents didn't choose to divorce because of you or to ruin your life, like Emily said. I'm sure they agonized over their decision because of not wanting to hurt you or make things difficult for you.

It's very difficult to start all over at a new school, but I'm also certain that you can pick yourself up and start over. Jump in. Make some friends. Try out for a sport or something else of interest. If you spend all of your time wishing you could go back, you'll miss out on what God has for you ahead.

"For I know the plans I have for you," declares the LORD, "plans to prosper you and not to harm you, plans to give you hope and a future."
JEREMIAH 29:11 NIV

Nothing Nice to Say?

Q: *I hear my mom bad-mouthing my dad all the time when she talks to her friends on the phone, or even in person when she doesn't know I can hear her. I'd always thought they were happily married, but now I wonder if she really does think he's that worthless. What can I do about it?*

~Meg

NATALIE: Oh, I would hate that, too. My parents are divorced, and they're still really careful to never bad-mouth each other—they work together to keep things nice for my sister and me. In your case, I'd be worried that your mom has bad feelings toward your dad that he doesn't know about. In reality, though, women sometimes do talk like that and think it's harmless. Think of friends at your school—some of them backstab and point out the flaws of others even though they're friends. I think they do that to make themselves feel better. Maybe your mom is dealing with something like that. It's really hard to say from here, so you should talk to her about it.

NICOLE: You know, I have to admit that I was like that once upon a time. I thought that's what women did. We gossip and man-bash. I thought there was no funnier topic than the dumb things my hubby did. That's until I started seeing it through his eyes, seeing him through God's eyes, and seeing him with the adoring eyes of my children. In God's eyes, he can do no wrong. In my children's eyes, he is perfect. So who am I to laugh at his weaknesses when he could burn me at the stake for mine?

Meg, pray for your mom that she would grow to see your dad through Jesus-colored glasses and love him the way He does and the way you do. It takes time, but the Holy Spirit can work a change in her heart and help her grow sickened by cheap shots and jokes at your dad's expense. When you're ready, have a talk with her and let her know that it hurts your heart to hear those things as much as it would hurt her to hear someone talking about you like that. Then give her a hug. And find your dad; he could probably use one, too.

Be friendly with everyone. Don't be proud and feel that you are smarter than others.
ROMANS 12:16 CEV

Target Practice

Q: *My parents only had one kid—me. My dad always wanted a son, but he's stuck with a girl. He wants me to go hunting with him and shoot at animals. I don't think it's okay to shoot animals for sport. I think it's okay to kill them for food, but not just for fun. How can I get out of this without hurting my dad and creating even more distance between us?*

~HAILEY

EMILY: Have you tried talking to him and telling him how you feel? What if you wrote him a letter or showed him this page? I think it's really important that you're honest with him. He might not have any idea you're feeling like this.

NICOLE: There are a couple of things going on in that question. First, there's the philosophical issue of hunting for sport. It's a perfectly rational viewpoint to feel uncomfortable with the idea of killing animals just for fun. I get that. It's not for everyone, and I actually share that feeling with you. The other part to your question is about connecting with your dad in some way.

I think you need to separate those issues into two different conversations, two completely different issues. Your stance on hunting can be just that. You can believe that, live that, even try to spread that position even if your dad disagrees and does his own thing when it comes to hunting. You can simply tell him your viewpoint and then drop it at that. You don't have to convince him or even get him to like your thoughts. But you should be yourself on this issue. Don't go hunting just to make him happy—that would never be fulfilling to you anyway.

As for your relationship with him, I agree with Emily and think you need to be open with him. Let him know that you sometimes feel inferior to what he wanted you to be and that you'd like to find a way to connect with him. He may not want to go shopping or go for pedicures, but maybe he'd like to go to an amusement park or a car show. There are plenty of things you can enjoy together. It just might take a bit of work to find them.

> *Be devoted to one another in love. Honor one another above yourselves.*
> ROMANS 12:10 NIV

He Said/She Said

Q: *My parents fight constantly. Sometimes I think it would be better if they just got a divorce. I don't know if I even want to get married if this is what it's going to be like. I want to talk to my dad and mom but don't know how to begin the conversation. Help!*

~JENNIFER

EMILY: Divorce is usually not the best option. It's never a perfect solution because a lot of pain is involved in the split. I know this for a fact because my parents are divorced. There are definitely some good reasons they're divorced, but it's not always easy. There might be something going on between your mom and dad that you don't know about, so you should talk to them about it. They need to hear how you feel about the fighting.

You mentioned that you aren't sure you want to get married one day because of your parents' relationship. You can make things very different for yourself by choosing your husband very, very carefully. Pray for God to help you find the one He has for you, and then to help you do what it takes to have a happy life together.

NICOLE: Talking to Mom and Dad is a great plan. Divorce is rarely the best or only option. They need to know how you feel and how their fighting affects you. They may not even realize that they're hurting you. Maybe family or marriage counseling would help, or maybe they could talk to their pastor.

Whatever they decide, they need to have all of the information so they can make a good decision about what to do. A big piece of that puzzle has to do with how you feel about your home life.

As far as how to begin the conservation, I've always found that being direct is the best plan. If you feel like you simply cannot handle the conversation yourself, consider asking a pastor, youth leader, or other trusted adult to help you through it. And be sure to spend some time in prayer before you talk to them. Ask the Lord to prepare their hearts to receive what you have to say.

Cast your burden upon the LORD and He will sustain you.
PSALM 55:22 NASB

A Gift from God

Q: *I'm fifteen, and my mom is pregnant. I'm kind of grossed out by it and totally embarrassed. I haven't told any of my friends, but it's going to be pretty obvious soon. What should I do?*

~ALYSSA

NATALIE: When I found out my mom was going to have triplets a couple of years ago, I was ecstatic! I couldn't wait to experience having those little babies to hold and love, and I was proud of my mom for what she was doing. I don't think there was ever a moment that I felt grossed out or embarrassed. I did feel worried, though; I just wanted everyone to be okay.

I think you should be thinking more about how your mom's doing and that you're going to have a new sibling soon, and not be so worried about what your friends think. Who cares, really? That baby is coming—might as well jump on board and enjoy the journey.

NICOLE: Ouch. I guess, as a mom who had triplets three years ago when Natalie was ten, I feel a little stung by that question. I understand that at your age, everything is about what your friends think, but this is taking it a bit too far, in my opinion. Alyssa, your mom is carrying your brother or sister. Someone who will be a part of your family, love you, and look up to you for the rest of your life.

It's all a matter of perspective, and I want to caution you not to do anything or say anything that you'll regret one day. This could be a beautiful, wonderful time for your family, and this baby is a precious gift. Enjoy it!

> *Lo, children are an heritage of the LORD: and the fruit of the womb is his reward.*
> PSALM 127:3 KJV

The Perfect Sister

Q: *I'm pretty good at everything I like to do. I get decent grades. I have a good number of friends. Then there's my sister! She is perfect. The most popular girl in her grade. Prom queen. Straight A's. Head cheerleader. How on earth can I compete with that? I feel invisible next to her sometimes.*

~Alyssia

EMILY: At your age, getting good grades and having a lot of friends is great. As you get older, you'll find your own skills and talents. I've seen that happen with my sister. She didn't do much when she was younger except do well in school. Now she plays on the volleyball team and plays the clarinet really well. I look forward to this next year because I'm about to get involved in some things, too. Just give yourself time and keep your eyes open to find out what you're best at.

Don't sell yourself short by taking a backseat to your sister. Be yourself; I promise it's more than enough!

> *Each of you must examine your own actions. Then you can be proud of your own accomplishments without comparing yourself to others.*
> Galatians 6:4 GW

NICOLE: Ah, the perfect sister. What a pain! I'm sure Emily has felt like that at times, but it sounds like she's worked through some of the competitiveness and tried to find her own way. I love her advice about being patient until you figure out what really excites you. It won't do any good for you to try to be just like your sister. You're different people and the world only needs one of you.

Thankfully, God made each and every one of us different but special and beautiful in our own ways. You were made in the image of God just like your sister was, and I was, and Emily was.

No Guarantees

Q: *I'm only thirteen, but sometimes I feel like I have to be the grown-up. My parents both work a lot and I pretty much take care of the house and make sure there's some kind of dinner ready when they get home. They crash after dinner because they're so tired, so I do the dishes too. Sometimes it just doesn't seem fair, especially when I go to my friends' houses and see that it's not that way for them. What should I do?*

~CARALYNNE

EMILY: One night when your parents are home and you're having dinner, you should open up with them and let them know exactly how you feel. They can't help you figure it out if they don't know. As for your comparisons with your friends' families, God has perfectly chosen yours for you and will help you through whatever you face.

NICOLE: I answered this before Emily did, and I had to chuckle because I can imagine she'd say some of the same things. I work a lot, and I have a lot of little kids. That means everyone has to pitch in around here. It would be that way even if I didn't work so much or we didn't have the triplets, though. I believe in teaching responsibility and contribution. I think a family should function as a unit and everyone should participate to the best of his or her ability. It's the only way my girls will become godly wives and loving moms, and my sons will become strong, godly husbands and fathers. It's intentional to raise the family like that.

Also, you should realize that life bears no guarantees. Just as your mom and dad would prefer a life of luxury and leisure, they are doing what they need to do to provide for you and raise you the way they see fit. Without comparing your family to others, find the joy and goodness in your home, focus on that, and do your part.

Care about them as much as you care about yourselves.
PHILIPPIANS 2:4 CEV

The More, the Merrier

Q: *My mom and stepdad are talking about adopting kids from China. I'm not sure how I feel about this for a couple of reasons. First, our house doesn't have a lot of room. Second, I already don't see my parents enough because they're working all the time. And third, when you adopt kids from other countries, there's a lot that can come up. I'm not sure it's a good idea. They're waiting for me to tell them whether I'm on board or not. How can I decide?*

~Kristian

EMILY: This is kind of difficult to advise because adopting kids is such a serious and permanent decision. It's not really something you can try out and then change your mind. But I guess I'd have to ask, "What would Jesus do?" I think He'd make the sacrifices necessary to give some underprivileged kids a home and a family. I think you should support the adoption and learn to accept the idea of some new siblings. In the end, you'll be a better person for doing it.

NICOLE: Yes, I agree, Em. What a privilege! You must really have some awesome parents if they want to open their lives to some needy children. Amazing! Let me address your points one at a time:

1. Room. That's a temporary struggle. It's a concern that is mired in the material. I have a house with three bedrooms and six kids. Hubby and I share a room as do Natalie and Emily. Erik has his own room until he leaves for the air force pretty soon. The triplets share the living room—they don't even get a bedroom. But we're happy. I wouldn't trade it for the world.

2. Maybe having some needy kids to focus on as a family will give you all a renewed goal to make family time a priority. You may find out that you get to spend more time with them this way.

3. There's a lot that can come with anything—but nothing good is without sacrifice.

> *"Whoever receives one such child in my name receives me, and whoever receives me, receives not me but him who sent me."*
> Mark 9:37 esv

Broken Home

Q: *I have two questions. From what I've read about you, Nicole, I get the feeling that you're divorced and remarried. Is that okay for a Christian? And Emily, how do you feel about having a stepdad and half brothers and half sisters? What's great about it, and what's not so great?*

~JOYANNA

EMILY: It's not anything bad for me to have half brothers and sisters. I don't even think of them that way at all. I've never used the term "half" to describe them. They're just my brothers and sisters. I also don't think there's anything wrong with having a stepdad. I feel lucky that I have such a big family and so many people to love me and take care of me.

NICOLE: Honestly? No, it's not okay. God's plan for marriage is that a man and woman unite as one in a covenant with Him. Forever. Biblically, divorce is allowed for some very specific reasons—mainly adultery. Adultery breaks the covenant agreement, so God recognizes that as the dissolution of the marriage. But He then goes on to explain that remarriage is a problem sometimes, too.

Fact is, divorce in many (most?) cases is sin. I do think there are other things that can break the covenant of marriage, but God usually asks the believer to stay in the marriage anyway. I'm grateful for my divorce because I believe we are both happier people. I don't regret it, necessarily—even

though there may not have been biblical grounds. I have sought forgiveness and healing for the poor choices I made by perhaps choosing someone God hadn't okayed for me, and for the things I did to contribute to the breakdown of the relationship.

In the end, as with any sin, we repent; God forgives; we move on. I wouldn't say that it's okay to do something against God's will, such as divorce, knowing you can be forgiven, but forgiveness is available for each and every sin in our lives—past, present, and future. While I'm not proud of the mess I helped make of my marriage, I'm thankful for God's grace and for fresh starts.

> *If you, LORD, kept a record of sins, Lord, who could stand? But with you there is forgiveness, so that we can, with reverence, serve you.*
> PSALM 130:3–4 NIV

Family Matters

Q: *This weekend is my grandparents' sixtieth wedding anniversary party and we have to travel a few hours away to get to it and will be gone all weekend. A lot of relatives are flying in from out of state, and my parents are superexcited about it. The problem is, I have a lot of plans this weekend and would rather they let me stay in town with a friend. They said it's up to me. What should I do?*

~ALI

EMILY: Well, there's no way my mom would let me miss an event like that if it weren't for a good reason. I mean, don't you think it would be kind of hurtful to your grandparents and other relatives if you don't go? I think you should just do it. The weekend will be over so fast and you'll have made some memories, not to mention made some people pretty happy.

NICOLE: You didn't say how old you are, and that might make a difference to me in some cases, along with what your plans were. There's a big difference between staying back because you're committed to a softball tournament versus staying back to hang out at the mall with friends.

I'm kind of surprised your parents would even consider letting you skip such a big event where you'd see family you haven't seen in a while and be part of such a joyous occasion. And to be honest, I think it's rather selfish that you'd even want to.

Look, I don't mean any offense at all—I was your age once and I felt the same way about family functions. But now I'd give anything to have my grandparents back so I could celebrate them and be with them. Nothing would stand in my way of giving them that time and just being able to soak up their presence.

> *Grandchildren are the crown of grandparents, and parents are the glory of their children.*
> PROVERBS 17:6 GW

Sister Sitter

Q: *My older sister is married and has two kids. Just because I'm only fifteen and "don't have a life," as she says, she thinks it's okay to use me to babysit and not pay me. She thinks, as the auntie, I should want to. Well, I do want to play with my nieces, but not sit at their house until midnight—hours and hours after the kids are in bed—every single weekend. What can I do about this?*

~NELLY

EMILY: I can understand that you want to play with your sister's kids, because I would want to, too. Every weekend would get annoying to me, though, too. What if you told your sister how you felt and offered to babysit on certain days, a couple of times a month. Then just say no when she asks other times. It's okay to say no. You might find that a few weeks of doing that is too much when you realize how much you miss the kids!

NICOLE: Oh, this is a pretty easy one, as far as I'm concerned. You're a person and your time is valuable to you. You're just as important as your sister and her plans. She chose to have children; now it's her responsibility to take care of them. Period.

That being said, aunties are famous for being great babysitters, and I'm sure you love the kids and they love you. That's why it's very important to fix this situation now so you don't grow bitter and pull away completely. You need to set your boundaries. Decide when you want to babysit and, if you want to be paid, how much you think the job is worth. Kindly but firmly let your sister know that you want to be a part of their lives and that you want to help her out, but that it's going to have to be more on your own terms.

This is a good experience for you. I've sort of allowed myself to get taken advantage of by people over the years. I wish I had learned how to assert myself at your age so I'd have been more equipped to do it as an adult. I still fight my natural tendency to just let people use me—but I'm getting better. Fight that tendency and protect yourself.

Always be humble and gentle. Be patient with each other, making allowance for each other's faults because of your love.
EPHESIANS 4:2 NLT

Blessing in Disguise

Q: *I am adopted and have never met my birth mom. I really want to know her, or at least meet her, and my adoptive parents say it's fine with them if I try to find her. The only problem is I'm afraid I might hurt my mom and dad if I find my birth mom and have a relationship with her. What should I do?*

~CHARITY

EMILY: If you really want to meet your birth mom, and your adoptive mom isn't upset by it, you should try to find her. If you're successful and you want to get to know her better, you should work hard to make sure your adoptive parents don't feel pushed aside. They've done a lot for you and love you very much, so it's good that you're thinking about them now.

> *Hope deferred makes the heart sick, but a desire fulfilled is a tree of life.*
> PROVERBS 13:12 ESV

NICOLE: Yeah, it's definitely a good thing to reach out and learn about your heritage, especially since you have your adoptive parents' blessing. Why not go for it? Take it one step at a time and pray that the Lord opens doors that He wants you to walk through and closes the ones He doesn't.

Once you do find your mom, assuming you're able to, you might be tempted to keep your parents out of it all to protect their feelings. If you do, they'll feel like you're pulling away from them and worry that you don't need them anymore. Be sure to keep them up to date on the details—involve them as much as possible. Just keep them informed and let them in to the extent it's comfortable for you all.

111

WHAT NOT TO WEAR?

What to Wear?

Q: *My mom is always on me about what I wear. She won't let me wear any shirts that show even a fraction of my stomach, and I have to actually bend over in jeans to prove to her that nothing shows in the back, if you know what I mean. She even says there's stuff in the Bible about the way to dress right. Is that true? What should I do to change her mind?*

~DEANNA

NATALIE: Your mom is right to be concerned—she probably wants to keep you from growing up too fast. She's just working extra hard to make sure you don't turn into someone you'll regret one day. Also, people expect you to act a certain way that goes along with your appearance. I'm sure your mom wants to help you stay strong in your actions as well as what you wear.

NICOLE: Well, Deanna, you asked about what the Bible says about it, so here you go:

1 Timothy 2:8–10 (NKJV): "I desire therefore that the men pray everywhere, lifting up holy hands, without wrath and doubting; in like manner also, *that the women adorn themselves in modest apparel, with propriety and moderation.*"

Proverbs 11:22 (NKJV): "As a ring of gold in a swine's snout, *so is a lovely woman who lacks discretion.*"

God made you beautiful and it's a shame not to let that beauty shine. When you're indiscreet, it's like saying you're not worth protecting, not beautiful, not special. Let me ask you, whose attention do you hope to get by dressing immodestly? Let's be honest: You're seeking the attention of boys, right?

Matthew 5:27–28 (NKJV): "You have heard that it was said to those of old, 'You shall not commit adultery.' But I say to you that *whoever looks at a woman to lust for her has already committed adultery with her in his heart.*"

Romans 14:13 (NKJV): "Let us not judge one another anymore, but rather *resolve this, not to put a stumbling block or a cause to fall in our brother's way.*"

For all of you who were baptized into Christ have clothed yourselves with Christ.
GALATIANS 3:27 NASB

Itsy-Bitsy, Teeny-Weeny

Q: *My parents won't let me wear a bikini, even a conservative one. I think it's totally dumb—all my friends do. How can I change their minds?*

~Zoie

EMILY: I think your parents have their reasons. They probably just don't want you showing that much of your body. My sister and I aren't allowed to wear bikinis either—but I don't really want to anyway. I want to be able to really have fun and not worry about losing a piece of my bathing suit. Would your parents allow a tankini? It covers more and lets you have fun and be active without worrying that it's going to come off or rise up. I love them!

NICOLE: Good point about the tankini, Emily. If that's not an option for you, Zoie, it's really isn't a big deal. There are supercute one-piece suits out there. The most important thing is that you respect your parents and not go against their wishes, which are only meant to protect you.

In our home, the girls are allowed to wear a tankini, but not a bikini. To me, when girls wear a bikini, they might as well go swimming in their panties and bra. And some of the ones I've seen are even more revealing than panties and have only a tiny string holding them up. Your parents see this kind of thing going on and just had to draw the line where it was comfortable for them.

And, really, what are you hoping for by wearing a bikini? Showing as much skin as possible, at the expense of your parents' wishes, doesn't seem like a good trade to me. There's just no real need for that kind of immodesty, even if all of your friends are doing it. Be the classy one who shows up at the beach in a great one-piece and has a blast!

> *And I want women to be modest in their appearance. They should wear decent and appropriate clothing.*
> 1 TIMOTHY 2:9 NLT

Better Attention

Q: *I have friends whose parents let them wear stuff that mine won't let me wear—like really tight shirts with low necks and stuff. The boys in my class are always giving them attention. I know my parents are right, but I often feel jealous of the attention the other girls get. How can I get over these feelings?*

~LAYLA

NATALIE: I know what you mean. It's weird to think that boys are looking at our bodies like that, though. Don't you think? I don't like to wear low-cut tops because it sort of creeps me out that someone is looking. . .*there*. I guess I don't think that type of attention is anything to be jealous of. It's just boys acting stupid and girls leading them on for attention. You should rise above that and just ignore it.

NICOLE: Right on, Nat! Perfectly said. If boys are paying extra-special attention to girls just because they dress immodestly, what kind of boys are they? Do you really want that kind of attention, Layla? Much better than that is to wait for a nice, respectful guy who will appreciate you for who you are, not for how much skin you reveal. It's sad that girls feel the need to put themselves on display and cheapen their bodies and reputations just to get a few looks and comments. That's certainly not love.

It really is creepy that these boys whose attention you want probably still have a teddy bear hidden under their pillows. Okay, maybe not to

that extreme, but you guys are young. You don't need to worry about body parts and who gets attention for what. Just be modest, respectful of your own body, and aware of the risk of causing temptation or lust. Boys are visual creatures and are really affected by what they see. Don't put them at risk for sin by being around them in clothing that will lead them to lustful thoughts.

For ye are bought with a price: therefore glorify God in your body, and in your spirit, which are God's.
1 CORINTHIANS 6:20 KJV

117

Christian Costume

Q: *I want to wear the same clothes all the popular kids wear, but as a Christian I'm supposed to be modest. How can I fit in without sacrificing my modesty?*

~BETH

EMILY: It's great that you see how important it is for a Christian to really think about how she dresses for school. If people won't hang out with you or don't like you because you don't have the best clothes, you don't want them for friends anyway. I think it sets a good example when someone who is known to be a Christian is different from other kids who are flashy or immodest.

NICOLE: The way you dress says a lot about you. It tells people how you want to be seen and even with whom you want them to identify you. It can lump you into a category or separate you from people. Since you're talking about modesty, let's look at some of the trends. Short skirts and shorts, tops that show a bare midriff, low-cut shirts, bra straps showing, etc. These are all ways to tell society that your body isn't sacred. It's there for all to see, and you have no reason to hide or protect it. It says that you're willing to use your body to get attention. And it speaks volumes to the fact that you don't care about the message you're sending.

On the other hand, appropriate clothing that covers things that should be covered and is respectful of your body demands that others respect it, too. You'll have a much easier time saying no to certain peer pressures if you start right by presenting yourself as a person who respects herself.

Your adornment must not be merely external—braiding the hair, and wearing gold jewelry, or putting on dresses; but let it be the hidden person of the heart, with the imperishable quality of a gentle and quiet spirit, which is precious in the sight of God.
1 PETER 3:3–4 NASB

FREAKS AND GEEKS

Gleek

Q: *Hi. I'm a sophomore this year. I've never done anything extra like a sport or band. I kind of want to try out for the school play this year, but I'm afraid my friends will think I'm weird. My parents told me to do it if I want to and not to worry about what other people think. But that almost assures me it's a dorky thing to do. I mean, if it weren't, they wouldn't have just said that, right? What should I do?*

~Misty

NATALIE: I have somewhat of a similar situation. I'm absolutely in love with student council, but none of my friends are doing it this year. I don't want to be surrounded by a bunch of people I don't know and who aren't even in my grade. The friends I have who are doing it this year are in office (president, VP, etc.), so I wouldn't get to hang out with them anyway. I haven't decided for sure what I'm going to do. I'm trying to get one of my friends to do it with me, but my plans are to go for it regardless of what my friends do. Who knows, Misty? Maybe we'll both make some new friends this year.

NICOLE: Teams, groups, musical instruments. . .those are wonderful ways to express yourself and grow. I'm never one to tell a teen to overcommit to things like that, but participating in one or two special extracurricular activities is great!

Who cares what other people think? Even if they tease you for a little while, they'll get over it when they come to the play and see how awesome you are!

Acting in plays, singing, even dancing can bring joy to a lot of people and offer entertainment to crowds, not to mention the unity that develops among the cast and crew.

I really hope you do it. You might be uncovering a talent that you didn't even know you possessed—or maybe you did know, and now it's time to show it to everyone else. Step out of that comfort zone and just go for it! When you get a little nervous, remember that God made you just the way He wanted you. Ask Him for confidence to use your talents.

> *Whatever you do, work at it with all your heart, as working for the Lord, not for human masters.*
> Colossians 3:23 niv

Wonderfully Made

Q: *The kids at school treat me like I don't even exist, and I always feel lonely. What can I do to make friends or have others notice me in a good way?*

~Maddy

EMILY: The most important thing I want to tell you is that you shouldn't change yourself just to make kids like you. If you want to make friends, you should be a friend to everyone. Approach kids, talk to everyone, and reach out to people who are hurting or lonely like you. Be willing to start the conversations and step out of your comfort zone. It's always a risk to reach out because you might get rejected, but you always fail when you don't try.

NICOLE: Oh, Maddy! I am so sorry you feel this way. The teen years can be so difficult because of these sorts of things. I'm sure you've heard stories about how the best supermodels started off awkward and gangly, and how your inner beauty is the most important thing. While I agree with those comments, I realize that's not what you're asking here.

Can I be perfectly frank? If you're down on yourself, if you're moping and slinking off to be alone, you're only causing more of the same stuff to happen. It's time for you to stand proud and be confident. Take control instead of giving so much power to people who only want to hurt the weak. You're probably saying, "Right. That's easier said than done." I get that. Really, I do. But this is a perfect time to fake it until you make it. Pretend you're in a play and your role is the confident, beautiful, popular head cheerleader. Carry yourself through school just like she would, and eventually, maybe not immediately, but soon enough, people will start to show you more respect and you'll see a big change.

> *Charm is deceptive, and beauty is fleeting; but a woman who fears the LORD is to be praised.*
> **PROVERBS 31:30 NIV**

> *I praise you because I am fearfully and wonderfully made; your works are wonderful, I know that full well.*
> **PSALM 139:14 NIV**

Solitude

Q: *I'd rather be alone most of the time than with a bunch of people I have to try to make conversation with. Is something wrong with me just because I don't have a ton of friends and don't like big, noisy groups?*

~SIMONE

EMILY: I don't think so at all. You are who you are. I like to be with big, noisy groups sometimes, but other times I need some peace and quiet. I think we all have times when our needs are different. You should just do what makes you happy and know that neither way is right or wrong, or even better.

NICOLE: Interesting question, Simone. I think the key to my answer is going to be that you said, "I'd rather. . ." You're not saying that you wished you had more friends or a busier schedule. You like the way you're doing things and just want confirmation that it's okay, right?

Of course it's okay! No two people are alike; God did it that way on purpose. How boring life would be if we were all exactly the same. Extreme extroverts need to be around people all the time. They're uncomfortable when they're alone and don't quite know what to do with themselves if they aren't in the center of a group.

On the other side, introverts prefer quiet, space, and alone time. They get anxious if too many people are around and often need to break away from groups to find a quiet place. You can be at either extreme, or somewhere in the middle, and be exactly who God designed you to be. Don't let other people tell you how you should be or what's normal and not normal. Be yourself, meet the needs of your heart and soul, don't push yourself to be someone you aren't, and don't think for one second you're inferior to people who are different than you.

For you created my inmost being; you knit me together in my mother's womb. I praise you because I am fearfully and wonderfully made; your works are wonderful, I know that full well.
PSALM 139:13–14 NIV

Good, Clean Fun

Q: *My friends sometimes tease me for being a Christian and assume I won't do anything fun. How can I have fun with my friends but still be a witness to them and still be accepted by them?*

~KAMI

NATALIE: I have gone through this same situation multiple times. It's not about being accepted—that's not the main goal. The main goal is that you stand up for what you believe in and defend your faith and your choices. It's okay to be friends with non-Christians, and that's what God calls us to do so we can lead people to Him. However, it's also important to have friends who share your faith and who will support you as you stand firm.

NICOLE: The very best time to deal with this issue is before you actually face it. It's much easier to build a good reputation than to try to repair a bad one. It's also easier to be accepted for who you are when it's not a pressure-filled moment. Better that your friends and peers know you well enough that they know ahead of time what you believe and what you'll do in a situation, than for you to try to defend your choices in the heat of the moment.

You might be past that point though. If so, you're going to have to stand firm and endure whatever teasing they throw at you. Crying, whining, arguing—those things only add fuel to bullies' fires and encourage them to keep

at it. If you smile and say something confident, assured in who you are, the pleasure they get from mocking you fizzles.

One last point: you said your "friends" sometimes tease you. Are you sure those are your friends? Maybe this is a good time to reassess your relationships and consider finding some friends who share and support your values.

But in your hearts revere Christ as Lord. Always be prepared to give an answer to everyone who asks you to give the reason for the hope that you have. But do this with gentleness and respect.
1 PETER 3:15 NIV

UGH! . . . FRUSTRATIONS!

Out of Focus

Q: *I'm fifteen, and I'm frustrated. I have a seven-year-old brother and my mom recently got remarried to a man with a three-year-old and a four-year-old— both boys. I get asked to babysit a lot; I get paid for it, and they say I don't have to do it, but they'd just hire someone else, and then it would be like I had a babysitter. Also, I feel like my whole life is about little boys. I'd just like to have one day that I didn't have to step around cars, racetracks, and piles of building blocks. I tell my mom and step-dad that I need some time alone, but they tell me that I have my own room and should be satisfied. What do you think?*

~Katrina

NATALIE: I can relate to your concern about babysitting. After I talked to my mom about it recently, she was able to show me how I wasn't really seeing it clearly. With all of my activities out of the house, and the time the babies sleep, it would be impossible for me to actually babysit more than an hour a day, but I wasn't even doing it that much. I realized that I had overreacted. I suggest that you try to keep track of just how much you actually do babysit and see if it's really as much as it seems like.

NICOLE: Nat has great input on this question because it's real for her, too. I can honestly tell you, though, that I've tried to make a real effort not to take advantage of my girls. I would guess that your mom thinks you want to babysit and earn money. So be careful about resenting things you've agreed to or would miss if they were gone. Sounds to me like your mom would be happy to hire a sitter and let you off the hook. Give that a try and see how it works. You never know, you just might miss the cash.

Do your best to present yourself to God as one approved, a worker who does not need to be ashamed and who correctly handles the word of truth.
2 Timothy 2:15 NIV

Always Broke

Q: *My friends always want to do things like going to the movies or shopping, but I never have any money. Do you have ideas for ways I could make some extra cash?*

~ALYSON

EMILY: I feel the same way. Everything is so expensive that a few-dollars-a-week allowance barely keeps gum in my backpack. I can't wait until I'm old enough to get a real part-time job. Some ideas are babysitting, cleaning, working at a local store, or tutoring younger students after school.

NICOLE: Those are good ideas, Em, but one reason there's no gum in your backpack is because you go through it so fast! *wink*

Alyson, there are tons of things you can do. In the summer you can help neighbors with yard work, wash cars, clean windows, walk dogs, etc. In the winter, there are always people looking for help shoveling snow. Babysitting is a pretty standard option. If you haven't yet, you can take a babysitting course at your local community center—you'll learn safety skills that will help you get jobs over other girls who haven't taken the course. You can also ask your mom or dad for extra chores to earn some money.

Be sure to plan ahead about what to do with the money once you earn it. How much is for sharing? How much for saving? How much for spending? You want to make sure you're starting good, godly habits for money management now. Figure out how much you're going to give to the church. Ten percent is recommended, and start with that right off the top. Then you want to save a portion of everything that comes in. After you've taken care of those two things, the rest is yours to spend as you wish.

> *And whatever you do, do it heartily, as to the Lord and not to men.*
> COLOSSIANS 3:23 NKJV

Math—Ugh!

Q: *I'm homeschooled and everything is so easy for me! Everything except for math. I get so stressed out when it's time to work on math that I itch a lot, I have trouble breathing, and I have to blow my nose. My mom tells me that I have a bad attitude, but I really don't mean to. I'm trying, but she says that it's not good enough. I don't mean to sound like I don't like my mom or anything. I love her with all of my heart, but still. What should I do?*

~Grace

EMILY: Maybe start off with some easier problems and then advance every day until you get to something new. If that doesn't help, maybe you should talk to your mom openly about it when you're not under pressure. She can probably help you if she knows exactly what you're dealing with. And maybe take a break from math for a week. Then, when you come back to it, start with something you fully understand, and then build from there so you can figure out where the confusion and frustration set in.

NICOLE: I totally agree. I even think a combination would be great. If you could take a week off and then come back to it with the help of a tutor, you would do great. And I always think an open conversation with Mom and Dad is a necessary part of solving any dilemma.

The other necessary part to solving a problem is prayer. You really should pray about this struggle and let God help you as you study. The girls and I prayed for you just now.

Just know, Grace, we all have something that we struggle with. Math happens to be my weakest subject, too. Other people struggle with English; for others it's spelling. It's hard to study the things that don't come easily to us, but that's probably where we need to put our focus most. Hang in there. You're a bright girl—you'll do fine! Write us anytime if you have questions!

> *For I am the LORD your God who takes hold of your right hand and says to you, Do not fear; I will help you.*
> ISAIAH 41:13 NIV

Charge It!

Q: *I really love to shop. It seems like even when I have new clothes that I've only worn once or twice, I want something new. Sometimes I can't even sleep because I'm trying to find ways to come up with the money to buy the newest things. And since they're new, they aren't on sale, so they cost the most. Once they're on sale, I don't like them anymore. My mom gives me money a lot, but it never seems to be enough. I babysit and do chores to earn money, but it takes a long time to earn enough money to buy the kind of things I want. Should I get a job?*

~Rachel

EMILY: What if you have a garage sale to help you earn some money to buy new clothes? Or have you ever heard of Plato's Closet? That's a store where you can turn in your old things and get credit for new ones. They might not be the newest clothes on the shelf, but they'd be something different for you to wear if you're bored with the things in your closet.

You could also make a deal with yourself that you have to wear your clothes a certain number of times before you buy something new. That will cut down on the trips to the mall and keep you from spending too much.

NICOLE: Rachel, I understand what you're dealing with. I went through the exact same thing when I was your age. You've already learned the most important part of your lesson: It's. Never. Enough. You already know that you're never going to be satisfied with material things—there's always something more to reach for. There will always be something new at your favorite store.

Do you know why they put the new things right up front and why they don't go on sale right away? For people just like you who are getting trapped by the desire for more and more new stuff. Ask yourself:

1. What does God say about worldly goods? (Matthew 6:20–21)

2. What does God say about priorities and contentment? (1 Timothy 6:7–10; Hebrews 13:5)

3. How does God see *you*? (1 Samuel 16:7)

And my God will meet all your needs according to the riches of his glory in Christ Jesus.
Philippians 4:19 NIV

Something Special

Q: *I want to do more with my life, but I don't have any special talents or any-thing really unique to offer. I help in the nursery at church sometimes. I try to help out at home. But I want to do something big—something that will really make a difference. How can God use someone as "non-special" as I am?*

~CHERYL

NATALIE: In God's eyes you're very special and unique. He made you just the way you are for a real purpose that only you can handle. You should try out some different things and see if you have talents or interests you didn't know about. You never know what you might find out about yourself. Does your church have a music program or a puppet ministry? Those are some great ways to try out skills.

NICOLE: Great point, Natalie! That actually happened to me. I had no idea that I would be any good on the radio—no idea at all (and many might say I'm not). But it sounded fun, and I knew I'd never know unless I tried. So I went for it. I can't even being to explain how nerve-racking it was to open my mouth to speak on the air the first moment of my first show! But it turned out to be kind of a natural thing for me, and whether I'm great at it or not, I love it and know that God has called me to it.

There are tons of things you can look into, Cheryl. What do you like to do? If you like music, learn an instrument. If you love to read, maybe you'll find that you have a knack for writing. If you enjoy studying the Bible, maybe you'd be great at leading a small group or teaching others in some way. You should pray about this desire you have and ask God to show you direction.

And whatever you do, do it heartily, as to the Lord and not to men.
COLOSSIANS 3:23 NKJV

Touchdown!

Q: *I'm a girl and I like to play football. I'm not huge by any means, but I am strong enough to hold my own and I'm not afraid. Do you think it's okay for a girl to play on the boys' football team?*

~ERIKA

EMILY: I think so. Lots of boys think that if girls do things that are supposed to be for boys only, it's wrong. But I think girls should have the freedom to do what they want to do as long as they don't expect the game to be changed to fit them in.

NICOLE: Yeah, I don't know that it's a matter of right or wrong from a moral standpoint. What are the school rules? What do your parents say? Why do you want to do it? Those are all the questions you need to be asking yourself.

If it's not against the rules, your parents are in support of it, and you're doing it for the right reasons, then I say *go for it*! If your motives are just to prove something to someone, and you have to battle with people to make it happen, then I wouldn't be supportive of that choice. No good can come out of making waves just for the sake of causing a stir. But I'll never say that you shouldn't follow your dreams or passions for the right reasons.

God knew exactly what He was doing when He made you the way you are and gave you the talents and interests you have. He didn't make any mistakes, and He delights in you—just as you are. So, assuming it's allowed in your school and your parents are in favor of you doing it, go have fun. . .and show those boys how it's done!

> *But in fact God has placed the parts in the body, every one of them, just as he wanted them to be.*
> 1 CORINTHIANS 12:18 NIV

So Not Fair!

Q: *My friends get a lot more allowance than I do. I only get $5 a week. What do you think is a fair allowance?*

~MEG

NATALIE: In my situation, I don't get a specific allowance. I. . .um. . .get whatever I want. Ha-ha. I'm kind of joking, but really, my parents do provide everything I need and a lot of wants. They give me cash to go places and money when I need clothes and stuff for school. I don't ever feel like I'm deprived. I say all of that to make you stop and think. Do you have a similar situation and need to step back and look at all your parents do for you? If so, the $5 is probably a pretty fair amount.

If you don't feel that applies to your situation, consider what your parents are able to do. Sometimes financial strains mean that's the best they can do, and you should be grateful for any amount in that case.

NICOLE: Good question. I really don't think there's an answer to "fair allowance." It depends completely on your family. Your parents have to decide what they can afford based on their income, bills, other children, etc. Even if I said $50 a week was a fair allowance, if they don't have it, they can't give it. So before you make a big deal over the amount of money your parents give you, find out how they arrived at that number.

Instead of asking for a bigger handout, see if you can find more ways to contribute to the family by raising your own spending money. You can earn some cash for yourself by babysitting or doing other things that pay.

Remember, your parents are doing the best they can and are trying to do what they think is best for you. I agree that $5 doesn't go very far these days, but I also think that allowance is an extra, not an entitlement. Many entire families get by with far less than that per week. Be thankful for what you have.

> *Don't love money.*
> *Be happy with what you have.*
> HEBREWS 13:5 GW

Girly Times

Q: *At my church the youth pastor only seems to plan events that are geared toward the guys. How can the girls get a say in what we do?*

~Jody

EMILY: I'm not really sure what you mean. Most events that would be enjoyable to both boys and girls are ones that aren't too girlie or too boyish: games, sports, and activities like golf, bowling, skiing, etc. I think you just need to be open with the youth pastor and show him with proof what you mean. Maybe write down a list of the recent activities and show him how none of them really appeal to girls. Ask him if you can rotate guy/girl events or even let your girlfriends plan a few.

NICOLE: That's a good idea, Emily. I'd also have to ask you, Jody, what are you considering to be "girl" events over "guy" events? Typically, in a co-ed group, it's difficult to do really feminine things like spa days or shopping trips. Thinking back to my youth group days, I can't imagine the boys sitting still for pedicures!

Like Emily mentioned, the events have to be sort of neutral, which may seem more appealing to the boys than to you—but everyone might not feel that way. And if your youth pastor is male, it's logical that he's pulling from his experience and interests. Offer to help him plan, and then try to get your two cents in.

When I was young, once a year the boys and girls split up for a special event. The boys went away for an overnight on a Polar Bear Campout and did all that outdoor guy stuff. The girls had a Teddy Bear Camp-In and stayed in a hotel in downtown Chicago and went shopping and sightseeing. Maybe you could try to organize something like that for the group. But when you're all doing something together, just remember that it really needs to appeal to everyone and not be specifically girlie.

I can do all things through him who strengthens me.
PHILIPPIANS 4:13 ESV

Waterworks

Q: *I think I'm a pretty happy person. People even call me perky. But sometimes I feel like crying—and I have no idea why. What causes that, and what should I do about it? Is something wrong with me?*

~Kristin

NATALIE: It occurs to me that you might be trying too hard to be what people assume you are, and you are missing what you're really feeling down deep. In your question, you pointed out right away what people call you—perky. Are you too focused on meeting those expectations and not getting your emotional needs met? The teenage years are full of lots of changes, and you need to give yourself space to feel things and grow as you face them. I definitely think you should talk to a trusted friend or advisor about what's really going on inside of you. Open up and let the real you out.

NICOLE: Welcome to adolescence, Kristin. I'm sorry to say that's one of the trials your body is going through as your hormone levels change and you mature into a woman. It's totally normal, even though it feels strange and might even make you feel like a crazy person. Just trust that it's normal and will pass.

That being said, Natalie made a fantastic observation and I think you should follow that advice. Also, if you feel your sadness, anger, or any other emotion is to a dangerous extreme, you need to involve a parent or trusted adult immediately. If you have ever had thoughts of hurting yourself or someone else, that's a different situation than the normal hormone-induced emotional swings and must be checked out by a doctor right away.

> *Let the peace of Christ rule in your hearts, to which indeed you were called in one body. And be thankful.*
> Colossians 3:15 ESV

135

You're Hired!

Q: *I want to make some extra money babysitting this year. What do you think would make me a really great babysitter, and what should I not do?*

~Courtney

NATALIE: I love to babysit. It's a great way to make extra money and help people out. The best quality of a good babysitter is being willing to give all of your attention to the children you're taking care of. That means no texting, phone calls, or visitors. Also, you shouldn't ever arrange a situation, like taking the kids to the park, just so you can hang out with your friends there. Parents really love it when they come home and homework is done and the kids are clean and either ready for bed or in bed. Your goal is to make the parents' day easier, not harder.

NICOLE: Natalie makes some great points! I babysat often as a teen, and I've hired plenty of babysitters in my years as a mom. One thing sticks out in my memory of my young years as a sitter. I messed up. . .big-time. The parents had gone out to meet some potential clients or to some sort of business dinner, and I was watching their four-year-old twins at their home. I fed the kids and got them to bed, then watched television. I didn't clean anything up in the kitchen or put away any toys. In fact, it never occurred to me to do that. A couple of hours later they came home with their clients!

They were so embarrassed about the state of the house and actually had a long talk with me about it later.

There are three main things I took away from that experience and that I look for in other sitters: keep the kids safe (be alert and aware at all times), give them a good time (no texting or Web surfing), and leave the house in better condition than you found it (do the dishes, fold a load of laundry. . .stay busy). If you work for the family for the hours you're being paid, then you'll leave a great impression and will have to start turning down babysitting jobs because you'll have too many.

> *Whatever you do, work at it with all your heart, as working for the Lord, not for human masters.*
> Colossians 3:23 NIV

Cinderella

Q: *I'm kind of thought of as a tomboy because I never dress up, and I like to play sports. I didn't mind the label so much when I was younger, but how can I change it now that I want to be seen as a girl and have people treat me like a girl?*

~RILEY

EMILY: I can relate because I have some friends who are definite tomboy-type girls. Now that we're getting a little older, they're starting to dress a little more girlie and they sometimes get teased for it. One of them gets really bothered by the teasing; the other just brushes it off and presses forward with trying to change her image. The thing is, they're trying to completely change into people they aren't, in my opinion. They won't play sports or hang out with the boys at all anymore. I think that's a mistake.

NICOLE: "Tomboy" is a label people put on you based on your appearance and actions. It's not a bad thing, and being girlie isn't a better thing. It's just different. If you're reaching a point in your life where you want to be seen as more feminine, you need to look deep inside yourself to see if you're ready to carry out a more feminine style. In other words, you can't just tell people to treat you more like a girl—you have to actually act more like one. If you want to.

Dress, speech, actions, friendships, hobbies—all of those things are ways you can tweak your image. I agree with Emily, though. Don't try to become someone you're not. Be true to yourself, or you won't be happy.

> *"For the LORD sees not as man sees: man looks on the outward appearance, but the LORD looks on the heart."*
> 1 SAMUEL 16:7 ESV

Think before Speaking

Q: *In dealing with people in authority like parents and teachers, how can I explain things or make a point without sounding argumentative or disrespectful? Why do authority figures sometimes assume they know what you are thinking?*

~TIA

EMILY: If you disagree with something someone is saying, it's important to show respect while you try to make your point. You need to keep your voice calm and the expression on your face should be humble, not mad. You can even come right out and say, "I'm saying this with all respect. . . ."

I think that they assume they know what you're thinking, or cut you off before you speak, because they think you're going to argue and don't want to hear it. You can avoid some of that by keeping your cool and politely asking them to hear you out.

NICOLE: It's not good to be dismissive or presumptive, but sometimes people with more experience than you may feel they know what you're thinking because they just might. But again, I'm not saying it's okay to cut you off or dismiss your thoughts. I'd really have to hear both sides to know the best answer to this, though. Would your parents say that you're argumentative or belligerent when they offer correction? If so, it may be less that they don't want to hear what you're saying, and more that they don't like how you're saying it.

A gentle answer turns away wrath, but a harsh word stirs up anger.
PROVERBS 15:1 NIV

Watch your tongue and keep your mouth shut, and you will stay out of trouble.
PROVERBS 21:23 NLT

Moving On

Q: *How do I deal with people in my life who have hurt me deeply and caused me a lot of problems? If I can't get over it, what am I supposed to do?*

~Tenisha

NATALIE: In his book *Teen to Teen*, Ron Luce says that forgiveness doesn't mean you have to be okay with what someone has done to you; it means you choose to lay down your right to strike back. To me, this means that forgiving someone doesn't mean you have to accept the bad actions or the hurtful stuff in your past; it just means you put aside your desire to get even.

NICOLE: It might sound cliché, but you just have to let go and move on. I know that's so much easier to say than it is to do, but it's what we're called to do as Christians. When God calls us to do something, it doesn't mean we're already equipped to do it, but it does mean that He's here to help us out.

Forgiveness is a big deal to God, and it requires faith to offer it when we don't feel like it. That's what a step of faith is, actually. It means lifting that foot with the intention to move forward, and then planting it on uncertain soil, trusting that there will be solid ground. Sometimes to heal relationships, it takes a step of faith—a gesture of forgiveness, an outreach of friendship, an effort of some kind—to make the first step toward restoration.

Sometimes people simply aren't responsive to offered forgiveness and want no part in restoration. That's okay. You have acted in faith; you've done your part. You can move forward with your head held high.

Don't repay evil for evil. Don't retaliate with insults when people insult you. Instead, pay them back with a blessing. That is what God has called you to do, and he will bless you for it.
1 PETER 3:9 NLT

HONESTLY!

When the Truth Hurts

Q: *My friend and I did something wrong and then both lied to our parents about it. My question is because I feel really guilty about it and actually want to tell my parents. If I do, they'll know that my friend was involved and will probably want to tell her parents. What should I do? I mean, is it fair to get her in trouble just because I feel guilty?*

~Marissa

NATALIE: If you feel guilty about what happened and it's nagging at you on the inside, you should tell your parents. If you're worried about your friend, you can ask your parents not to tell hers. But if your mom and dad won't agree to keep it a secret, you should talk to your friend first and let her know that you're about to tell the truth. Give her the chance to be honest with her family before they find out some other way.

NICOLE: First of all, I'm so glad to hear your conscience is bothering you. It means you have a soft heart and that the Holy Spirit is convicting you. Other than the obvious advice of not doing something to make yourself feel guilty in the first place, the best advice I have is to be honest. Listen to what your heart is telling you and keep yourself clean from sin: lies, disobedience, etc. Your parents might punish you for whatever you did, but it will actually build their trust in you that you had to fess up because they'll know that you're open to God's gentle prodding in your heart.

I agree with Natalie that you should tell your friend first. That way, she'll have the option of either doing the same thing and telling her parents— or taking a chance that your parents won't. Hopefully she'll decide to come clean, too.

> *The LORD. . .likes everyone who is honest.*
> PROVERBS 11:1 CEV

To Lie or Not to Lie?

Q: *This is just a basic question and isn't really about anything specific in my life. I was just wondering if you thought it was ever okay to lie about anything.*

~CARLY

NATALIE: God is clear that lying is a sin, but it would be difficult to go through life without ever telling a lie. For example, when someone's in danger or you don't want to hurt someone's feelings. I feel like those lies are almost acceptable or understandable at least. If someone asks you if she looks fat, you might not want to come straight out and tell the whole truth. But you also don't have to tell a complete lie, either. You can be truthful without being hurtful.

I don't think it's ever okay to lie just to keep from getting into trouble. If you did something wrong, you're going to make it even worse by lying, and I would say that type of lie is wrong in every case.

NICOLE: It might surprise you to hear there are plenty of examples in the Bible where people lied. Sometimes those lies even seem to have been blessed by God. Think of Rahab, who lied to save the lives of the Israelite spies in Joshua. Even though she was untruthful, it was to save lives and honor God. She is later mentioned as one of great faith in Hebrews 11.

There is also the modern example of wartime situations where people have lied to save lives. But there are as many other stories of people who chose to remain truthful in the face of the threat of death, and God saved them miraculously. He is capable and powerful to do that, so there is no situation that *requires* you to lie. If God wants to intervene, He will. That being said, I believe that He understands our weaknesses, asks us to trust Him, but knows that we will fail at times.

I agree wholeheartedly with Natalie, though. If the lie is because you want to avoid getting in trouble or to escape a commitment of some kind, it's wrong. Every time.

> *"Who may ascend the mountain of the LORD? Who may stand in his holy place? The one who has clean hands and a pure heart, who does not trust in an idol or swear by a false god. They will receive blessing from the LORD and vindication from God their Savior."*
>
> PSALM 24:3–5 NIV

Home Alone

Q: *My mom works all day, and during the summer I'm home alone from early in the morning until 6:00 at night. I'm not supposed to have any friends over while Mom's not home, but sometimes my friends just show up at the door. I admit, I let them in sometimes because I'm so bored. We don't do anything wrong while they're here, and it's not like I'm sneaking out of the house or anything. We just watch TV or lay out in the sun. I even have dinner ready when Mom gets home so she doesn't have to do it. I feel guilty, but it's really not bad, is it?*

~OLIVIA

NATALIE: Having friends over when your mom doesn't want them there isn't a great idea. What if someone got hurt or something got damaged? Try asking your mom for permission to have company sometimes. I'd probably say something like, "Mom, what if you had no contact with the outside world all day long? You wouldn't like it either." Just be sure if you say something like that, you smile while you say it or she'll think you're being snarky.

NICOLE: Aha! So that's how you work, Natalie.

Yes, I agree with the suggestion of being open with your mom about how you feel. I promise, she's not trying to make you feel lonely, and she's not trying to ruin your summer. She's just worried about you. Even though you might be too old for a babysitter, it's tough for a parent to let go and not worry when she can't be around much. It also sounds like your mom might be a single mom. (If I'm wrong, sorry for jumping to conclusions.) If so, she has a lot of pressure on her and doesn't need to worry about what's happening at home when she can't be there. Just be honest with her about how you feel, but you really, really need to be obedient and trust that she knows best.

> *"Whoever can be trusted with very little can also be trusted with much, and whoever is dishonest with very little will also be dishonest with much."*
> LUKE 16:10 NIV

Tattletale?

Q: *I can't even believe I have to ask this question, but I found out my dad has a girlfriend and is cheating on my mom. I'm totally positive that I'm right—I've double- and triple-checked my suspicions, which are now facts. Do I tell my mom? If so, how?*

~GABI

NATALIE: Normally I would recommend that you talk to a school counselor or someone you trust. But in this case, I think this is a very private thing and you should keep it to yourself until your parents are able to deal with it. Talk to your dad first and see how he responds to the accusations before you go to your mom. The truth has to come out, but nothing will be the same once it does. You're really in a tough spot, and I'll be praying for you and your family as you face what you have to do.

NICOLE: Oh, Gabi, I'm so sorry you have to face this. I'm going to assume you're right and have really confirmed this—you seem to realize that it's not something you want to accuse your dad of without knowing for sure. As for what to do, there is another option besides telling your mom right away. I recommend that you talk to your father and let him tell her. At least give him the chance to own up to it. Not only will it be better for the two of them if it happens that way, but it also will keep you from having to be the one to tell your mom.

Caution: he will probably deny it. If so, let him know that you will be going to your mom with what you know, unless he does first. If you're wrong, he can sort that out with her. If you're right, she deserves to know.

Before you do anything, pray for them.

> *Trust in the LORD with all your heart, and do not lean on your own understanding.*
> PROVERBS 3:5 ESV

Fess Up

Q: *I have a big problem. I told a lie and now my friend and I are fighting. She wants me to tell the whole class what I lied about, and she said if I didn't do it, she will never be my friend again. What should I do?*

~KRISTA

EMILY: If you told a lie, even if you're nervous to admit it, just do your best and go ahead and get the truth out. It's hard to own up to the things you do that are wrong, but you'll feel so much better after it's over. It's really hard when things like that are hanging over your head. Just do it fast, like pulling off a bandage, and it will be over.

Things like this happen at my school all the time and they never last long. People forget fast!

If your friend is important to you and her friendship means a lot to you, then you should do the right thing.

NICOLE: Emily's right. We all find ourselves in a tough situation like this at some point in our lives. We regret a choice we made and have to do something very difficult to get out of it. I want to encourage you to do what's right. Lying is never okay, and it's even worse if someone else gets hurt. So let your friend know that she means enough to you that you're willing to suffer embarrassment and ridicule for a short time.

But more important than your friend is God's forgiveness. Make sure you have a talk with God and repent of your dishonesty. Ask Him to help you be strong in the future and only let truthful things come from your mouth.

> *"Whoever can be trusted with very little can also be trusted with much, and whoever is dishonest with very little will also be dishonest with much."*
> LUKE 16:10 NIV

Against the Rules

Q: Hi! I'm sixteen and have two little sisters—one is three and the other is one. I'm a cheerleader and in band, so I don't have a lot of time to help with baby-sitting and stuff like that. My mom and dad hire my friend to babysit when I'm not going to be around. The problem is, my friend usually has her boyfriend come over while my parents aren't home, which is totally against the rules. I don't know if I should tell my parents. If I do, my friend will lose her babysitting job and probably get in trouble, because I'm sure my mom would tell her mom. Plus she'd be really mad at me.

~BETH

NATALIE: I think you need to tell your mom and dad. It's not okay that they are hiring your friend to protect their children and she's bringing a guy into the house that they don't even know. In my opinion, this is an easy one. You know what you need to do.

NICOLE: Beth, I commend you for caring. I also understand that it's hard to do things that you know will make your friend angry with you. However, she's really not taking into consideration the position she has put you in. You know that your parents would never allow her to have a boy over while she's babysitting, and even if they would (which I doubt), they deserve the right to check out anyone who's coming into contact with their little ones. In this case, the boy who's coming over is an unknown to them. That's not fair, and it's not safe.

Furthermore, if your friend is preoccupied with her boyfriend, she's not paying as close attention to your siblings as she should be. If something

happened and one of them got hurt, you'd feel horrible that you might have been able to do something to keep it from happening.

Hear the instruction of thy father, and forsake not the law of thy mother.
PROVERBS 1:8 ASV

Double Wii

Q: *We got a Wii for Christmas and my brother and I play it all the time—sometimes we argue over who gets to choose what we play. My friend's dad recently won an entire Wii system in a raffle and he offered me his used one. I'm going to stay at my friend's house this weekend, and they're expecting me to take the Wii home with me. Should I tell him we already have one and let him give it to someone else? Or should I just say thank you and bring it home so my brother and I can each have one?*

~SERENA

EMILY: Nice problem to have! Even though you could use a second Wii system, you should tell him you already have one. Thank him for thinking of you, but let someone else benefit from his gift. You and your brother can work out a schedule for the times you get to choose the game, the times he gets to, and the times you play it alone. And also, find a game you both like a whole lot and involve your whole family.

NICOLE: No fair! I don't even have one Wii. Maybe your friend's dad can send it to me! Just kidding. Really though, Emily is totally right. I'd definitely let him know that you have one already and that you assume he had wanted to give it to someone who doesn't. It's the honest and unselfish thing to do. Then, if he insists you take it anyway, you'll feel much better about it. He probably won't, though—if he thought two game systems per household were needed, he'd keep it himself.

Plus, you know, you and your brother really should be able to work this out. You have lots of times in life when you have to find ways to work with other people and share things. The ways you deal with that now will help you cope with the bigger situations later in life.

Give freely and become more wealthy; be stingy and lose everything.
PROVERBS 11:24 NLT

Come Clean

Q: *I saw someone cheat at school, and she wound up getting an A on a very hard exam that I had to study extra hard for. Should I tell the teacher about what she did?*

~Colleen

EMILY: Wow, that's a tough one. That has to be pretty upsetting. I think you should probably tell a teacher. If someone doesn't put a stop to it, it'll just keep getting worse. If a teacher gets involved, it might help that person not do something like that again in the future; plus it will make things fairer.

NICOLE: I'm actually not a big fan of tattling. It all comes down to motives for me. Do you want to tell on this person because you're jealous that this cheater got a better grade than you? Or do you think it really will help the teacher, the student, and the future of the class if the truth comes out? Really examine your heart and find out why you want the teacher to know before you run off and do something like that.

In no way am I saying that cheating is okay or that there shouldn't be a punishment. But I don't always think people should take it into their own hands. I always recommend that you go to the person who did wrong, in this case the cheater, and talk to her about how what she did makes you feel. Ask her to come forward and admit to her wrongdoing herself.

In the end, you're going to answer for your behavior, not hers. Jealousy is just as wrong as cheating. If you're unhappy with your grade, study harder next time.

The Lord. . .delights in people who are trustworthy.
Proverbs 12:22 NIV

Gambling with Life

Q: *My older brother hangs around with friends who gamble a lot. He's losing a lot of money and has started borrowing from me. I just found out today that he stole money from my mom's purse. What should I do?*

~Julia

EMILY: Your brother needs to know that what he's doing is bothering you. If he keeps doing it, you need to let your mom know so she can help him.

NICOLE: Ick. Gambling. What a waste! You know, God calls us to be good stewards of (that means to use wisely) the money, things, talents, etc., that He provides for us. Gambling is not a good way to use the Lord's money or our time.

That aside, when a person goes into debt to gamble, or worse, steals in order to gamble, he has a problem. This isn't one you can handle on your own. It's time for an intervention. You need to involve your mom and together have a talk with your brother. Let him know how worried you are and that his actions aren't okay. Your mom should tell him that the next time he steals, she'll call the police. But then she needs to follow through. It may be the only way to save him from a complete downward spiral.

Gambling is a stronghold, and once it gets into a person's life and takes over his heart, it's difficult to pry them away. You need to pray that God would loose its grip on your brother so that he can see clearly and break away completely.

> *For the love of money is a root of all kinds of evils. It is through this craving that some have wandered away from the faith and pierced themselves with many pangs.*
> 1 TIMOTHY 6:10 ESV

Just Words

Q: *My parents don't know I swear—but I do a lot. Not around them, of course, but with my friends and even when I'm alone. Is it really wrong? They're just words. If it is, how can I stop now that it's a habit?*

~AMBER

NATALIE: I was friends with a girl who swore all the time. Her entire vocabulary consisted of swear words. I tried to look past it for a while, but eventually it became too much for me to take. We aren't friends anymore and that's one of the main reasons. They are only words, but words show what's in your heart. As a Christian, your heart should be so sensitive to those words that you don't want to hear them, let alone say them. If it isn't, pray that the Holy Spirit would make you see how ugly it is and then help you stop.

NICOLE: After Jesus was crucified, Peter was accused of being a follower of Christ. In order to convince the people he wasn't, he cursed. The people knew Jesus wouldn't talk like that, so that was all the proof the people needed to believe that Peter wasn't a Christ follower.

How about you? Do you want people to assume you aren't a Christian because of your language? Is it really so important for you to talk that way that you're willing to risk your witness and the impact of your testimony for Christ?

Rather than being so concerned about those words you shouldn't be using, turn your focus instead to the wholesome and honorable speech that is evidence of the work of the Holy Spirit in your life.

> *Do not let any unwholesome talk come out of your mouths, but only what is helpful for building others up according to their needs, that it may benefit those who listen.*
> EPHESIANS 4:29 NIV

Untrue Love

Q: *My best friend has been with her boyfriend for a long time and they're really serious. He is amazing to her, and she loves him a lot. Recently I found out that he has cheated on her several times. What should I do? I think she should know, but I don't want to hurt her.*

~ALYSON

NATALIE: In this situation, I do think you need to make sure your friend finds out. If you feel okay with it, I think you should confront the boy first. Let him know what you know and give him a chance to come clean with his girlfriend. If he won't do it, then you need to tell her. It's not fair that this is going on without her knowledge.

Love must be sincere. Hate what is evil; cling to what is good. Be devoted to one another in love. Honor one another above yourselves.
ROMANS 12:9–10 NIV

NICOLE: First of all, she does need to know. Secondly, it's not you who has hurt her—it's him. It's such a shame that teenagers have to face such big issues at such a young age. This is one of the reasons it's so important to hold off on the physical stuff until marriage. It's too easy for one partner to stray when there's so little responsibility or commitment required before entering a deep relationship.

You're a good friend for taking care of her and making sure she isn't hurt any more than she already will be. I pray that the Holy Spirit gives you the words to say and that your friend will open her eyes to what's going on and make a choice to move forward, away from this relationship and toward purity.

PARENTAL CONTROLS

Campus Life

Q: *Hi, girls. I was just wondering about something. I'm a high school student, but I already think I want to be a missionary one day. My parents think I should go to college first and then decide if I still want to do that. I don't think I need a college degree for it, though. I just want to get started. Do you know how it works?*

~Marnie

EMILY: Having a college degree would never be a bad thing, but maybe it's not for you. That's something you'll have to decide with your parents— just try to get as much information as possible before you decide. If you aren't sure if you'll need a degree, you should talk to other missionaries who are doing what you want to do. I'm sure there are all different kinds of missionaries—some probably have degrees and some don't. It would just depend on what you wanted to do. Maybe you'll need to know a foreign language; maybe you'll want to be a nurse. I definitely think you should listen to your heart and follow God's leading, but still respect your parents. They're only looking out for what they see as your best interest.

NICOLE: I agree that a college degree is never, ever a bad thing to have. It would open up so many more doors for you. However, God knows best. It's His leading you have to follow, even in the face of logic and what others think is best. But God would never call you to go against your parents. That doesn't always mean they'll be right, but He'll make a way for you to follow His path while still respecting them. There's no need to make this decision today. Just pray about it and stay open to whatever He might bring your way. Also, there are organizations where you can work as a missionary on college campuses. That might be a good option for you as a blend of the two. Check out Campus Crusade for Christ.

That is why we labor and strive, because we have put our hope in the living God.
1 Timothy 4:10 NIV

Do as I Say, Not as I Do?

Q: *My parents drink alcohol, but they tell me it's wrong. Am I supposed to follow what they say or what they do?*

~LINDSEY

NATALIE: The first word that popped into my mind was *hypocrite*—people who say one thing but do another. But as I think a little deeper about this question, I think there are a couple of things you need to consider. First of all, you're underage, so drinking alcohol is illegal for you, but not for them. Secondly, you're not ready to decide what your body can handle, but maybe they are. Third, a lot of people believe that alcohol is 100 percent wrong for Christians all the time, but others think that it's only wrong if you get drunk. So there's a lot to consider, and it doesn't all mean your parents are hypocrites. You should talk to them and find out where they stand on it.

NICOLE: Sometimes people, even though they know something is wrong, are struggling to overcome a particular sin. Some Christian denominations teach strictly against any alcohol at all, like Natalie said—even to the point of claiming it's salvation dependent. I don't teach that myself. I believe that the grace of God covers all of our human weaknesses—past, present, and future.

A great thing for you to do would be to talk to your mom and dad and ask them what their position is on the issue of sin and salvation, and particularly the subject of alcohol. Also, as Natalie pointed out, you need to remember that because you're still a teen, there are legal issues surrounding the choices of alcohol. Even if your parents believe it's okay for them to have a glass of wine or an alcoholic beverage now and then, it's illegal for you to do it, so in that way, it's wrong.

In the end, you need to listen to God. If you're unsure about the Bible's stance on a particular subject like alcohol, you can pray for clarity and err on the side of the better plan.

Everything is permissible (allowable and lawful) for me; but not all things are helpful (good for me to do, expedient and profitable when considered with other things). Everything is lawful for me, but I will not become the slave of anything or be brought under its power.
1 CORINTHIANS 6:12 AMP

Self-Discipline

Q: *I recently made the volleyball team after I argued with my mom and dad about trying out. I told them I had to do it or I'd die. They didn't want me to do it because I'm already so busy and my mom was afraid I wouldn't like it. They were right. I hate it! Now what?*

~MARISSA

NATALIE: Earlier this school year, I joined the cross-country team. Half-way through the season it got to be really challenging for me because of my asthma. I had trouble breathing when I ran and that made me one of the worst runners on the team. I felt a lot of pressure to stick with it, but I finally talked to my mom about it and she said that she'd support whatever decision I made. That actually made it harder for me to quit because I had to choose. I really just wanted someone to make the decision for me. Eventually, though, I had to do what I needed to do and I stepped off the team.

NICOLE: We've all been there. Fight hard for something we just *have* to have only to find out it's not quite what we expected.

- Do you not like it because it's a lot of work?
- What about it isn't what you expected?
- Have you played games yet, or have you only been to practices?
- Are you unhappy because of certain teammates?

If it's because it's too much work, I'd really encourage you to stick with it for a while. The best things in life are the things we have to work for. And if you haven't had any games yet, hang in there for a little while. The games are the best part! The team spirit, camaraderie, wins, and even losses are what make a team. It's an experience everyone should have. If your dissatisfaction is because of people on your team, I hope you'll be able to look past that. Everything changes and the people you can't stand today may work for you one day.

For the Spirit God gave us does not make us timid, but gives us power, love and self-discipline.
2 TIMOTHY 1:7 NIV

159

R-E-S-P-E-C-T

Q: *There's this nice Christian boy who goes to my church and is in my dad's youth group. He's fourteen, and he wanted to text me but I'm not allowed. They said I'm still a little young (eleven and a half) to be texting boys. I know they're right, but here's the thing: he's texting me and I told him he's not allowed, but he still does every so often. I told my parents about three weeks ago, but he did it again over the weekend when I was with his sister. What should I do?*

~CANA

NATALIE: Um. I can answer this one pretty easily. I wasn't allowed to text or receive texts from boys until I turned thirteen. I knew that if I did, I'd lose my phone privileges. Until that time, my mom did random spot checks of my phone. I wasn't allowed to delete my messages until I gave her the opportunity to look through the conversations, which she didn't do very often because I had earned her trust. But all that changed once I was allowed to text with boys. Now she checks my phone just about every day. I'm limited on who I can text and how much I can go back and forth with them. Does it bug me? Yeah, sometimes. But I get it; I really do. One day I know that I'll be grateful my parents have kept such a watchful eye on me.

But at eleven years old, this wouldn't have been an issue. If a boy continued to text me after being told to stop, my mom probably would have given me two options: I could make it stop on my own, or she'd do it for me.

NICOLE: Yeah, Nat's right on this one. This boy is disrespecting you and your parents. He's asking you, someone three years younger than he is, to disobey your parents and sneak around behind their backs. That doesn't sound like a nice Christian boy to me. I know you're thinking, "Oh, he doesn't mean anything by it." But, Cana, either he respects you or he doesn't. Trust me. He doesn't.

> *If you don't do what you know is right, you have sinned.*
> JAMES 4:17 CEV

Fourteen Going on Adult

Q: *I think I should be allowed to do more things like stay up later than 9:30 p.m. I also think I should be allowed to watch PG-13 movies—I am fourteen, after all. I would also like to be able to go out with my friends to the mall, to the movies, and other places like that without a parent's supervision.*

Do you guys deal with that, and what do you do? Sometimes I'm a little tempted to do things anyway, like watch the movies at my friends' houses or stay up and watch TV in my room after my parents are in bed. I don't do that usually because I respect my parents and don't want to disappoint them. . .but it's tempting.

~J.C.

NATALIE: I totally get what you're saying! One time I was at my best friend's house and she picked out a movie that I wasn't sure my mom would approve of. I called home and asked for permission to watch it. Mom looked it up online and read about it. She ended up saying no, but she really respected me for calling to ask. She even called me back to thank me and tell me how proud she was of me. I felt great for respecting her and it became one of those special things between us. I think it helped make her really trust me.

I think it's important to build and keep your parents' trust. Much more important than watching a movie or staying up an extra half hour. You won't be fourteen forever.

NICOLE: J.C., I really don't think I can answer this any better than Natalie

has. I'm a pretty strict mom compared to many, but I also believe in a lot of positive reinforcement that encourages my girls to continue to choose to do the right thing. I really am proud of you for the respect you show your parents and hope that will continue as the peer pressure mounts. Pray that God will give you the strength you need to stand up to the negative pressure and do what's right.

> *Children, obey your parents in the Lord, for this is right.*
> EPHESIANS 6:1 NIV

Honor

Q: *How do I respect the wishes of my non-Christian parents while still following God's will? Sometimes they want me to do things that I don't want to do and they don't like when I go to church. What should I do?*

~Emma

EMILY: If your mom and dad don't want you to go to church, you should start praying for your parents. Ask God to help them see that it's a good thing for you to be in church; even pray that they would have a change of heart and want to go with you. Since you're an example of Jesus to them, you shouldn't argue about this. It's important to respect them and show them that you'll honor them even when you don't agree with them.

NICOLE: Hmm. I'm trying to think of times when a parent's wishes might go against God's will. There aren't too many that I can think of. Parents typically want their teens to be respectful, noble, honest, kind, trustworthy, pure, and generous—all things that God wants, too.

If they don't go to church or let you go, that's okay. Church isn't a requirement for a Christian. God wants us to get together with believers and worship Him, but He isn't going to blame you for this decision. In fact, He'd much rather you respect your parents' wishes than dishonor them by going against what they want—as long as it's not sin.

If you're unable to be in church, pray on your own. Ask God to soften your parents' hearts and to lead them to Himself. Pray that your attitude of respect will be a witness of Christ to them. Try to hang out with Christian friends so they can help hold you up and be a good influence on you. Finally, pray that God will always lead you out of temptation so that you would maintain your witness before your parents and your friends.

Children, obey your parents in everything, for this pleases the Lord.
Colossians 3:20 esv

A Little Bit Country

Q: *My mom only wants me to listen to Christian music. I don't get it. What's wrong with rock, country, rap, or jazz music? Especially country music—some of it is even about Jesus. How can you tell what music is good and what is bad, and how can I convince my mom to let me listen to the good stuff?*

~STACIE

EMILY: The best way to tell if music is good or bad is to read the lyrics and really think about what they're trying to say. If you can't tell what it means, talk it over with your mom. But like anything, you want to fill your mind with things that honor God, not pull you away from Him. The more your mom sees you wanting to do that, the more she'll probably let you make your own music choices.

NICOLE: That's right. The Bible says that if you're not for Him, you're against Him. I'd say that applies to music, too. Music is a powerful tool—it reaches people in ways other things can't. That's why people choose their music to match their mood and couples choose "their song" to define their relationship. There are songs for marriage, songs for breakups, songs to celebrate birth, and songs to mourn death. Music can grip your heart and soul and really affect you.

It's important to understand what you're listening to and even the heart and intent of the singer or band. There's nothing wrong with having fun with music and enjoying a good song, but it becomes wrong when the singer or the song's message takes your eyes off God.

There is some fabulous Christian music available, and even worship music that sounds as contemporary and vibrant as anything you can find on a secular radio station. I guess I have to wonder why a Christian would want to spend time listening to something that doesn't glorify God. . .and maybe your mom wonders the same thing.

> *Let the word of Christ dwell in you richly in all wisdom; teaching and admonishing one another in psalms and hymns and spiritual songs, singing with grace in your hearts to the Lord.*
> COLOSSIANS 3:16 KJV

Fast Food

Q: *I've been studying the Bible about fasting and I think it's a great thing and could make me feel much closer to God. I want to fast, but I'm a diabetic and my parents are afraid I'll get really sick if I don't eat for a period of time. If I don't do it anyway, does that mean my faith is weak?*

~JENNIFER

EMILY: Personally, I don't think you should fast if you're a diabetic—especially while you're young. Even if you don't fast, you can study the Word, pray, and submit to God. It doesn't mean you have weaker faith because you don't fast; it means you're being wise and respecting your parents' wishes. They only want the best for you and are afraid you'll make yourself sick. God knows your heart and He likes that you even wanted to fast.

NICOLE: I really respect that you would love to be able to fast. It's a commendable thing to want to grow closer to Christ and to be willing to make a sacrifice to see that happen. However, not all teenagers or even adults for that matter can forgo food for any length of time. Sometimes it's just not healthy. You might wonder why God doesn't supernaturally protect a person involved in a fast, and I'm not saying He wouldn't. But that same argument could be applied to taking medicine or receiving medical treatment. Why bother doing it if God can heal and protect? No. He gave us brains, and it's good to use them. A disease like diabetes is directly affected both positively and negatively by the balance of nutrition in your system. Not eating is not a good plan.

But that doesn't mean for a second that you can't fast. Here's a list of some things you might consider giving up for a fasting period. I'm sure you can come up with others.

- The Internet
- Social media
- Television
- The telephone or texting
- Caffeine
- A night out with friends

So, whether you eat or drink, or whatever you do, do everything to the glory of God.
1 CORINTHIANS 10:31 GW

Sweet Sixteen

Q: *What do you think is a good age to start dating? I'm asking because my parents and I disagree about this. Actually, my parents even disagree with each other. Dad thinks sixteen, but Mom says seventeen.*

~LEANNE

EMILY: My parents say that you shouldn't date until at least sixteen. I agree with that. I think when you're any younger than that, you're not ready for it. But I guess it would be up to your parents to decide whether your age will be sixteen or seventeen, no matter what Mom and I think. When you're older, it's not going to matter that much, so I wouldn't argue about it. Waiting is better than rushing.

NICOLE: Yeah, Leanne, this one is totally up to your parents because my rule is that there is no set rule. Every teenager is different and a lot of factors have to be considered before I can decide if one of my kids is ready for dating or not. It's not simply an age. There's no way I can know if you're ready without talking with you and your parents to see if they have reason to doubt your maturity, commitments, and goals.

Also, there is nothing wrong with waiting. The longer, the better. The longer you can wait to have your first date, the less time you have to endure the heartache of breakups and rejections. Just enjoy your teen years and let them be a time when you're being developed into a strong, confident woman who doesn't depend on a boy in order to have good self-esteem.

In the meantime, use this time to build a good reputation for yourself so that when the time comes, you can attract godly men who are looking for a righteous woman. You might not think that matters now, but time flies and one day you'll be ready to choose your husband. Be sure you have your pick from the best of the best—he'll be the father of your children.

> *Give her the product of her hands, and let her works praise her in the gates.*
> PROVERBS 31:31 NASB

Rated "M"

Q: *I like to play video games that are rated "M." I'm twelve years old and my mom says it's okay. My youth leader asked me why I like to play games like that and why I'd want to put those kinds of images into my head. I don't think it's that big of a deal. What do you think?*

~MOLLY

EMILY: It's interesting that your parents let you play them; that probably makes it a little more difficult to say no. At least, I'd recommend that you not play those games all the time because they can kind of take over your life. And if you do play them, pay attention to what's happening in the game—you should really stop playing when you come across something that wouldn't be good for you or pleasing to God.

NICOLE: I think your youth leader asked you a great question. What is it about those games or those images that entice you? Why are the most popular games the violent and suggestive ones? There are other games that require as much skill but don't have the violent aggression that the mature games have. It's a wonder that Christians are able to watch and participate in those games without growing uncomfortable with what they're seeing and doing—the killing, gory violence, sexually explicit scenes, crude language, etc.

I believe with my whole heart that if you prayed for the Holy Spirit to show you if those games were beneficial to you, or even just okay, you'd begin to feel a little bit negative about them. If you asked for Him to convict your heart when you're participating in something you shouldn't be, you'd start to pull back until you didn't want to play them anymore.

It's important to feed your mind with things that honor God and fuel your spiritual growth, not detract from it. You're in a formative life period that will lead you into your adult walk with the Lord. Lay a healthy foundation with good choices and a strong commitment to God's will for you.

> *"Anyone who isn't with me opposes me, and anyone who isn't working with me is actually working against me."*
> MATTHEW 12:30 NLT

Foundations

Q: *My parents are trying to force me to go to Bible college for at least a year after high school. They say I can transfer to a regular college after that if I want to. I don't see why I should do that, though. Wouldn't it make more sense to pick a school and stick with it?*

~Tayte

EMILY: I think you should go ahead and try the Bible college for a year. Why not? Your parents have a good reason for it. They want you to grow closer to God while you're getting your education. What could be wrong with that? Besides, you might like it and find a whole new career path opened to you that you hadn't even thought of.

NICOLE: Hmm. A year of Bible college first? That's actually a really good idea. I might even consider making that a recommendation for my teens, too. Why not start off with some good Bible education? Also, I can see a benefit in avoiding some of the partying that goes along with a typical university experience. There's definitely an element of that, even at Bible college, but it's far less than at a traditional school. Also, the peer pressure would be much less of an impact at a Christian college.

As for picking a school and sticking with it, that's not a problem. Many, many students start off at a community college for a year or two before transferring to a bigger institution. Schools work hard to make that transition as smooth as possible. Just do your research and make sure that all of your courses will transfer. Sometimes it's better to work toward an associate's degree before transferring.

"For I know the plans I have for you," declares the Lord, "plans to prosper you and not to harm you, plans to give you hope and a future."
JEREMIAH 29:11 NIV

167

Gift That Keeps Giving

Q: *I have really long hair and all my friends love it. I want to cut it short and donate the hair to Locks of Love for people with cancer. My parents don't want me to do it because they think I'll regret it later. I don't see how I could regret helping people like that. My parents are leaving it up to me. What should I do?*

~SOPHIA

EMILY: It's a great idea to donate hair—I know several people who have done it. You shouldn't really go against your parents' wishes; they know you best. But since they're leaving it up to you to decide, I think you should go for it if you want to. Hair grows back, so it's not a permanent choice, but helping someone will feel great forever.

> *Don't forget to do good things for others and to share what you have with them. These are the kinds of sacrifices that please God.*
> HEBREWS 13:16 GW

NICOLE: Sophia, go for it! I think it's an awesome thing to do and something that will set an example for a lot of people, even your parents. You can grow your hair back, but maybe you won't even want to. Regardless, even if you miss your long tresses, I don't think that you'll ever regret making a difference in someone's life like you'll be doing.

Make sure your parents are really okay with your choice; then see if you can make it an event for them to share with you. Let them see how excited you are to do it, and then how thrilled you are when it's over. Whatever you do—never let 'em see you sweat!

Drug Test

Q: *I've done some pretty dumb things. I got caught drinking and even smoking pot. I lied to my parents a bunch of times, and I've been grounded forever. I snuck out of my house while I was grounded, and now my parents don't trust me at all. They even want me to take a drug test. I think parents should trust their kids, and a drug test is insulting. What do you think?*

~JULIE

EMILY: I can understand why your parents don't trust you. With the things you've been doing, why would they? They care about you and are responsible for your safety and health. The drug test is a smart idea so they can know what's happening in your life. I suggest you go along with their wishes and do the drug test or whatever else they might ask you to do to prove that you've changed.

NICOLE: I agree with Emily completely. I'm sorry that things have been rough for you, Julie, but you're really not in a position to be making demands or setting expectations for your parents. You can't force them to trust you; you can only change your ways and let them see the evidence of that change in your life. Over time, not immediately, their trust will develop naturally in response to what they see in you.

In reading your words, I sense some bitterness and anger toward them that you were caught in these things. That anger is evidence to me that you haven't truly repented of what you've done. Someone who is truly sorry turns from her ways and submits to the authority God has put in her life. If you really do believe that you were wrong and want to change, you should be honoring your parents and doing whatever it takes to gain back their trust. If you don't really believe you were wrong, then your parents are absolutely right to reserve their trust.

If we confess our sins, he is faithful and just to forgive us our sins, and to cleanse us from all unrighteousness.
1 JOHN 1:9 KJV

Double Standards

Q: *My parents are total hypocrites! They tell me that it's wrong to lie, but they do all the time. They tell me it's wrong to break the law, but they drive far over the speed limit most of the time. They try to tell me it's wrong to have premarital sex, but I know they did. What am I supposed to think of all of that?*

~JOLIE

EMILY: I think that your parents aren't perfect—just like you aren't. They want you to make better choices than they have in the past or do even now. I think it would be better if they didn't do those things, but since they aren't perfect, there would always be some other kind of sin to point out in their lives.

NICOLE: I can imagine how frustrating that "do as I say, not as I do" approach must be for you. It's difficult to make the right choices when you don't have great role models living the life in front of you, but it's still possible. Rather than listening to your parents to learn your rights and wrongs, follow the Word of God. Let that be your guide, and be an example of a godly lifestyle in front of your parents.

You'll find that people will fail you throughout all of life, so it's much better to let God be your moral compass because He never wavers.

Another thing I want to point out, Jolie, is that the choices your parents made before they got married happened a long time ago. Just like you have made mistakes in your life and then received forgiveness either from your parents or from God, they need that kind of grace in their lives, too. You really have no idea how they've worked through the issues of their past sins, and you shouldn't judge them for them. The fact is, premarital sex is wrong, and if they're telling you that, then they're right. If you have a question about their past, that's something you need to take to them, but it doesn't change the truth about the sin itself.

> *If you honor your father and mother, "things will go well for you, and you will have a long life on the earth."*
> EPHESIANS 6:3 NLT

Do Your Part

Q: *My parents make me do chores every day—stuff like doing dishes, sweeping the floor, or folding laundry. I'm really busy with my own life, though. Why should I have to come home and do that stuff, too?*

~HAYLEY

NATALIE: Preaching to the choir, sister! I completely understand your frustration and have dealt with the exact same thing. But I have to remind myself that my whole family is just as busy, and if I don't do my part, it will fall to my mom. If no one contributed, she'd be stuck with all of it. Everyone needs to participate and be a part of making the household work.

There have been times when I've been so busy I almost broke down and cried. I felt like I couldn't do my chores or be a part of my family. My mom has a talk with me when it gets to that point and tells me I have to cut something from my schedule in order to keep my priorities straight. It's hard to make those tough choices, but I'm always glad after I do.

NICOLE: I gave this question to Nat to answer because she's the busiest of the kids. With volleyball, church activities, friends, band, etc., it seems she always has something extra to do after school. But she still has chores. The deal is, those extra things are great as long as her grades are up and she's able to be a functioning and contributing member of the family. Chores are a part of that. If something started to slip, she'd have to decide what to give up to make more room. She doesn't want to lose her activities, so she makes it work.

Families are so busy these days, it's only natural to expect everyone to do her part. If not, it's all left on the shoulders of your parents to make everything function well. Your parents aren't expecting too much by making you contribute.

Children, obey your parents in everything, for this pleases the Lord.
COLOSSIANS 3:20 NIV

Alone Time

Q: *My parents will only let me go out on double dates. Why won't they let me single date? It's not like I can't do something wrong if there are four of us rather than two of us. How can I convince them to give in and trust me?*

~Becca

NATALIE: I don't think the goal here should be to get your parents to give in. Your goal should be that they'd have complete trust in the choices you make. But even with that, it's not always a matter of trust. My mom trusts me completely, but she still works really hard to protect me from temptation by keeping me out of situations that might make me struggle.

Maybe you should ask yourself why it's so important to you to go out on single dates. If you want privacy, maybe it's best you not have it.

NICOLE: That's the thing, Becca: Why do you want to be allowed to go on dates alone? What would you do differently than if you have another couple along? You know, your parents might be reacting to the same question. "Why does she want alone time with this boy? What are they planning or hoping to do?" Rather than arguing with them or trying to get them to give in, show them that it doesn't matter to you and that you're more interested in making good choices than in getting more freedom.

It's best to have a safeguard in place against temptation. If you keep yourselves out of situations where you're alone, you won't even have the opportunity to mess up.

Keep watch and pray that you will not fall into temptation. The spirit is willing, but the flesh is weak.
MATTHEW 26:41 GNT

Should I Stop?

Q: *I am in the seventh grade and have been with my boyfriend for over a year. His parents let us go to his bedroom alone, but my parents would be horrified if they knew. It's not like we're doing anything bad—we watch movies and kiss a little bit. Should I stop doing it?*

~COURTNEY

EMILY: Before you decide if you should stop, you should talk to your parents about it. I know you said they'd be horrified—but you should give them a chance to hear you out and look at the whole situation. If they are truly against it, then you should definitely stop. On the other hand, maybe they'll be able to help you figure out how to make it a better situation.

NICOLE: Yes! Yes! Yes! And I'm not only saying that because your parents wouldn't approve—that's obviously a factor, but it's not my biggest concern. Courtney, it's a good, good thing that you're asking this question—it shows that you have a desire to do the right thing.

Look, you've been with your boyfriend for a while, and you admit that your relationship gets physical sometimes. A bedroom is the wrong place for you to hang out. Really, the worst thing you guys could do would be to give yourselves privacy like that. It does nothing but set you up for challenges and temptations that you might not be able to withstand one day.

I want to encourage you to find alternatives to being alone in your boyfriend's bedroom. You could spend more time at your house where it seems your parents put on some tighter restrictions. You should also talk to someone like a youth leader or someone you can trust and ask for accountability on this issue. Finally and most importantly, set your own restrictions and stick by them. You and your boyfriend are ultimately the ones responsible for what you do. So determine now that you'll keep yourself from those tempting situations and then stick to your commitment.

> *"Watch and pray so that you will not fall into temptation. The spirit is willing, but the flesh is weak."*
> MATTHEW 26:41 NIV

Love Notes

Q: *My mom and dad found notes that my boyfriend and I had written back and forth to each other. They found out in the notes that we have a pretty physical relationship—even though we haven't actually had sex. They told me I can't see him anymore, but I'm mad because they read what I wrote. What should I do?*

~WHITNEY

NATALIE: In my life, everything is very monitored and open. My mom reads everything, or at least has access to it—like text messages, e-mails, Facebook chats, etc. I have no problem with this because I'm not hiding anything. I think it's good that I have that much protection because it will make me think twice before I ever do something wrong. So I think it's totally fair that your parents read your notes and are stepping between you and your boyfriend. In my opinion, you're focusing on the wrong thing by being angry at them.

NICOLE: I totally agree with Natalie. Your focus is on the wrong part of this, Whitney, and your anger is misplaced. Your parents had every right to read your notes; in fact, I'm so glad the Holy Spirit led them to do it. They must have been feeling some doubts or concerns about you that prompted them to check up on things. I think that's fantastic—and probably just in time.

You didn't mention how old you are, but as a teenager, unmarried, living in your parents' home, you shouldn't be in a physical relationship to that magnitude. Listen, I get it. I really do. I was just like you when I was a teenager. I enjoyed attention from boys and tried hard to feel accepted by them. I felt empty when a relationship ended and moved right into the next one immediately. I wish I had known then what I know now.

Early physical relationships only leave you feeling emptier. That's not what your soul needs, so it isn't satisfying. When you realize you're not satisfied, you'll reach for more and more, until you make a life-changing, irreversible mistake. Be grateful that your parents stopped you in time.

> *For the grace of God has appeared, bringing salvation to all men, instructing us to deny ungodliness and worldly desires and to live sensibly, righteously and godly in the present age.*
> TITUS 2:11–12 NASB

Home Alone

Q: *I'm in fourth grade and my parents are divorced. My mom lets me and my younger brother stay home alone while she's at work, but my dad thinks I should have a babysitter. What do you think?*

~JOSIE

EMILY: Since you're only in fourth grade and your brother is younger than you, I don't think it's a very good idea for you guys to be home alone for a long period of time. A little while is okay, but if it's too long, you might get into trouble or be at risk for bad things to happen. But even though I think that, and your dad thinks that, it doesn't mean your mom is wrong.

NICOLE: Actually, the choice for whether or not you have a babysitter is up to your mom and dad, so there's not a whole lot I can say to that. What I'd like to talk about is what you do when Mom and Dad aren't around. If you're home alone, how do you spend your time? What does your little brother do?

My encouragement to you is to focus on the role you have as the older sister and make it a priority to be a great example to your brother. He will follow your lead. If you're doing things you aren't supposed to or not following the rules your mom has in place, then he will find his own ways to break them, too. It becomes a slippery slope where no one wants to get caught, so secrets are kept and threats are made. You can avoid that mess by doing what you know is right.

Being a single mom is tough. Support your mom by being trustworthy and helpful. Then the question of whether you need a babysitter may answer itself.

> *Yes, just as you can identify a tree by its fruit, so you can identify people by their actions.*
> MATTHEW 7:20 NLT

Bleep!

Q: *I have a huge pet peeve. My parents are on me every day about my language, but they swear all the time. They try to pretend they hate swear words, but they say them when they talk to each other, when they're on the phone, when they drop something. . .all the time! Why should I bother cleaning up my mouth when they can't be bothered to practice what they preach?*

~Lauren

EMILY: Do you think it's wrong to swear? Do you think your parents are right to want you to stop? Right is right; wrong is wrong—no matter what everyone else does. You just need to decide if you're going to respect your parents and clean up your language because it's the right thing. Then you can pray for your parents to have the ability to do the same thing.

NICOLE: I can understand how that would be frustrating. Let's put your parents' language aside for a moment and just focus on yours. Why do you swear? What's the appeal? People who swear are often viewed as uneducated, unintelligent, and unmotivated. It's offensive and disrespectful to people you might swear around in public settings, and it isn't allowed in many places. Some wise thinkers have thought that people who swear must not be good communicators, because if they were, they'd choose better words to get their point across. So what is it about saying the words that appeals to you?

Now about your mom and dad: Have you had a heart-to-heart with them about it? Have you respectfully pointed out the hypocrisy and asked them to explain their thinking to you? As the child in the situation, though, you do need to respect your parents and obey them. You can use your clean, wholesome language to pray for your parents.

> *From the same mouth come blessing and cursing. My brothers, these things ought not to be so.*
> James 3:10 ESV

> *Those who guard their mouths and their tongues keep themselves from calamity.*
> Proverbs 21:23 NIV

THE PRESSURE'S ON!

Peer Pressure

Q: *Hi! I don't really need advice; I'm just curious about some things. Natalie, what are the things you struggle with the most in your grade? What kinds of things do you see other kids your age doing that you know you want to avoid and are surprised to see going on? What's the biggest challenge you've had to overcome when it comes to peer pressure or something like that? Nicole, what was the hardest thing for you when you were in school?*

~Lucy

NATALIE: For the answer to your first question, I think the biggest problem I face at school is the bad language. A lot of people, including myself, have been picked on for not talking like that. The important thing is to stay strong and not give in.

Your second question made me think of all the dating that goes on. I'm surprised by how many girls and boys my age think they need to be in a dating relationship and how many parents actually allow it. I mean, I'm in seventh grade! It's going to be a long time before I get married, so I don't see any need to start dating now.

The biggest peer pressure I've had to overcome so far is when my friends want me to watch movies I know I'm not supposed to watch. I've been able to stand up to them and stick to what I know my parents allow, but it's difficult sometimes.

NICOLE: Great questions, Lucy! I've sure enjoyed hearing Natalie answer them. Let's see, the toughest thing I dealt with in school? I'd have to say it was everything related to trying to be accepted and part of the "in" crowd. I did things that I wouldn't have done—things I knew were wrong—in efforts to be accepted. I believe that if I'd had a better self-image and hadn't tried so hard to please my friends, I would have stayed strong and avoided a lot of that. Sometimes it's not the individual action that's the real problem; it's the underlying motivation for it.

But now you must also rid yourselves of all such things as these: anger, rage, malice, slander, and filthy language from your lips.
Colossians 3:8 NIV

179

Living on the Edge

Q: *My older sister is dating several guys. She goes out and parties. She drinks and drives. Sometimes she even offers me alcohol, and I'm only fifteen. What should I do? How can I stay on the right path with a bad influence like that?*

~DANA

NATALIE: Step one: talk to your parents. Your sister is living dangerously, not to mention illegally. After that, you could go talk to the guidance counselor at school. You can do that anonymously and then the counselor will be able to reach out to your sister without her ever knowing it was you. Along with involving an adult, you can have a talk with your sister and let her know how worried you are and that you wish she were a better influence on you. And make sure you make good choices—don't let your sister's bad decisions influence yours.

NICOLE: Great answer, Natalie. Dana, you're not responsible for what your sister does; you're only responsible for what you do. Please don't let her bad choices lead you down a wrong path. Instead, consider how badly you're feeling about her behavior and resolve never to go that route yourself. It takes preparation to stay true to those commitments. You need to decide now what you're going to do and say when you find yourself tempted or pressured to do bad things so you can stand up to your friends and say no to sin.

Now that we've covered you, let's talk about her. She is definitely engaging in some very dangerous behavior and your parents need to know. Normally, I suggest that people go to the person first before involving a parent or anyone else. In this case, I'm going to suggest that you go straight to a parent, immediately, and explain everything. Her life and the lives of other people are in danger. Still reading? Scoot!

Abstain from every form of evil.
1 THESSALONIANS 5:22 ESV

Stand Up and Stand Out

Q: *If I'm around other people my age who aren't Christians, is it okay for me not to tell them I'm a Christian and not really act like one either? I'm not saying I want to do horrible things; I just want to fit in.*

~SHELLY

EMILY: Being a Christian is an important part of who you are. If you have to pretend you're not one just to get other people to accept you, then that means they're forcing you to be someone you aren't. Do you really want to hang around those people anyway?

Also, how would it make God feel if you pretended not to know Him? Imagine if your mom was embarrassed of you and pretended not to know you around other people. Wouldn't that make you feel horrible?

NICOLE: Yeah, this is a big one. The Bible says that if you're ashamed of God, He'll be ashamed of you.

The truth is, if it's isn't Christianity that makes you feel different, it'll be something else. That's the nature of being a teenager. Instead of trying to be a follower and fit in to someone else's idea of who you should be, why not stand up stronger and be the example they can attain to? You may be thinking, "Oh, it just doesn't work that way in the real world." But I can testify that it is working that way in my girls' lives. Just a couple of weeks ago, when asked to give a speech about her hero, one of Natalie's classmates chose Natalie for the subject of her speech. She's making a difference and standing out in her public school for the right reasons.

I'm not saying she never deals with being teased, but she's wise enough to let it blow over, and it always does. After the words fade, she's left with a strong reputation and the respect of everyone—adults, teachers, and students. Consider how you could shift your thinking to being more like that, making you a leader rather than a follower, for Christ.

> *"But whoever denies Me before men, I will also deny him before My Father who is in heaven."*
> MATTHEW 10:33 NASB

Ups and Downs

Q: *Sometimes I do or say things because I don't want to deal with the teasing or pressure from my friends. Sometimes I'm able to say no, but sometimes I can't. Why is it so hard to be consistent in the Christian life as a teenager?*

~Gia

NATALIE: I totally get what you're saying. It's hard to be the one who's always swimming against the stream. There are all sorts of temptations and pressures around us, and there are all kinds of people who want us to fail in our Christian walk. They are watching and waiting for us to mess up. That's why it's so important to stand strong as a witness of our faith.

Consistency is the most important part of it because people aren't going to remember the times you said no; they'll only focus on the times you gave in. That's where your reputation will be built. Also, people love when they can label Christians as hypocrites. It doesn't matter that we're human, too; we're expected to hold ourselves to a higher standard, and people are watching.

NICOLE: Great points about reputation, Natalie. It's true that people kind of keep watch on Christians to see when and where they mess up. It's sad but true. Consistency in your commitment is important to your witness for Christ.

But you are human and you need to give yourself a little bit of a break.

Think of the apostle Paul. He said that there were lots of times he did what he didn't want to do and didn't do what he knew he should do. He admitted that he failed. The important thing is that you recognize you're weak and don't preach to others about your actions as though you're above them. Be real with people and with yourself.

Behave yourselves wisely [living prudently and with discretion] in your relations with those of the outside world (the non-Christians), making the very most of the time and seizing (buying up) the opportunity.
COLOSSIANS 4:5 AMP

Side by Side

Q: *If God doesn't want me to sin, why doesn't He just keep temptations away? It would be so much easier that way. It's almost like He's waiting for me to mess up.*

~RISSA

EMILY: When you think about doing things, the temptation is because you want to do them—not because God is tempting you. We're all sinners, and if there weren't any temptation, there wouldn't be any sin. And if we didn't have any sin, we wouldn't need a Savior. I don't think it's that He's waiting for you to mess up. I think it's more that He's waiting to pick you up when you do.

NICOLE: Well said, Em. Rissa, all you need to do is go back to the very beginning of the Bible, to the book of Genesis. God made a perfect world, a place of peace and harmony, a place without sin. It was when people fell for the temptations of the devil that sin entered the world and destroyed the harmony between God and man. The whole rest of the Bible—God's story—is about saving us from those choices. We mess up; then He swoops in with a way out and the grace to cover the sin.

Instead of asking God to keep temptation away, because in this life there will always be sin and the temptation to do bad things, pray that God will come alongside you and guide you through it—giving you the strength you need to stand up against sin and peer pressure of all kinds.

> *No temptation has overtaken you that is not common to man. God is faithful, and he will not let you be tempted beyond your ability, but with the temptation he will also provide the way of escape, that you may be able to endure it.*
> 1 CORINTHIANS 10:13 ESV

183

Tipsy Teens

Q: *One of the biggest dilemmas facing Christian teens today is how to handle the pressure to drink alcohol. Is it always wrong to drink? What should I do when my friends pressure me to do it?*

~LILY

EMILY: If you're a teenager, then yes, it is wrong because you're underage and it's illegal. If your friends are pressuring you to do it, just think about what the Bible says. Ask yourself what Jesus would do in that situation. Stand strong! Say no to alcohol and drugs, and be an example of Christ to your friends.

NICOLE: First, let's address the issue of adults and alcohol use. I have decided not to take a firm stance on this one way or another and direct you to your pastor. The thing is, from my searching the scriptures, I've found no reason to believe that moderate use (a glass of wine with dinner) of alcohol is bad. Many denominations feel differently, and I wouldn't want to convince you otherwise. I think it's pretty clear that overindulgence or misuse of alcohol is sinful.

As for underage drinking—it's illegal and clearly wrong. Not only could you get into a lot of legal trouble for doing it, you're also setting yourself up for the risk of long-term alcohol abuse. Please avoid it at all costs. Prepare your no right now so you're not caught off guard when your friends pressure you. It's much easier to say no and leave than it is to undo a bad decision.

Pray for strength in those tough moments. God promises to always provide a way through temptation if you trust Him to do it. Just say no!

For the grace of God has appeared, bringing salvation for all people, training us to renounce ungodliness and worldly passions, and to live self-controlled, upright, and godly lives in the present age.
TITUS 2:11–12 ESV

Spring Break

Q: *It's my senior year and all of my friends are going on a cool trip for spring break. My parents have already said I could go, but I know there's going to be a lot of drinking and partying. Should I go? If I don't go, what should I tell my friends? They'll think I'm crazy if I stay home even though I have my parents' okay.*

~Kalyn

NATALIE: I think it's okay for you to go on the trip—there's drinking and all kinds of stuff going on everywhere. The best idea is to find ways to protect yourself while on the trip. Stay with someone who supports you in your beliefs and who won't pressure you to do something you know is wrong. Talk about accountability ahead of time so she can help you stay on track—and then you do the same for her.

NICOLE: I really love that you're willing to stay home rather than face peer pressure and temptation. It makes me think you'd probably be able to stand strong even if you did go, in which case you'd be an example to your friends. However, you have to remember that if they get into trouble for drinking, you might be at risk, too. Also, you won't have a lot of fun as the only sober person among a bunch of drunken people acting stupid.

Are there other things you could plan ahead to do while the others are off partying? Or could you make sure there's at least one other person with the same values as you? Better yet, can you talk to the group about making the trip more healthy and legal, rather than risking it all for some drinking?

In the end, this is a choice you're going to have to make; I can't make it for you. I do like that you're willing not to go, and maybe that's your best bet. If you choose to go, decide ahead of time what you'll do when the pressure hits.

Do not set foot on the path of the wicked or walk in the way of evildoers.
Proverbs 4:14 NIV

185

Gold Medal

Q: *I've been in gymnastics for nine years. I'm really good at it and my parents have put a lot of money into my athletics. Now that I'm in high school, I just don't want to do it anymore. My parents were kind of counting on a college scholarship. Is it okay for me to quit?*

~CHERYL

NATALIE: I don't think the question is whether it's right or wrong to quit. The question goes back to priorities. If your family can't afford college and you truly do have the potential of earning the scholarship, then it might be selfish to quit. Also, take a look at how much time and money have been invested in your gymnastics. If you look at the grand total, it might make you feel differently about quitting and you might want to push forward and at least finish out high school.

NICOLE: I don't know—are you sure you want to? Don't you want to see it through to the end and see what happens? What are the reasons you want to quit? If it's so you can have more time to hang out with your friends, then I would encourage you to resist the urge. If it's so you can try other things and experience different sports, then maybe. I can't really answer this for you because I don't know the whole story.

A college scholarship might not be the right reason to stay in a sport, because anything could happen between now and college. Just realize, though, your parents may not be able to afford to foot the bill for college. If they can't, you'll have to find other means of raising tuition. Jobs, student loans, grants, scholarships—those are all ways to make it work. Just think that through before you come to a decision about gymnastics.

Be sure you talk to your parents about this, too. You can't know what they're really thinking unless you hear them out.

> *That the God of our Lord Jesus Christ, the Father of glory, may give you a spirit of wisdom and of revelation in the knowledge of him.*
> EPHESIANS 1:17 ESV

Bad News

Q: *I really like this one boy, but he's always texting me and instant messaging to meet him somewhere like the park or whatever. I tell him my parents won't allow it, but he wants me to lie to them. I just don't feel right about it, but I don't want to judge him. What should I do?*

~AUDRA

NATALIE: I've been in this exact situation. I was chatting on Facebook with a guy and he asked if we could meet somewhere. I told him I'd ask my parents; then I told my mom he was one of my other friends. Somehow, my mom felt like she needed to dig a little deeper and then found out the truth about where I was planning to go and who I'd be with. I really regretted that lie and I still regret it. It's really the only time I've gone against my parents like that, and I don't plan to do it again.

About this boy. . .if he wants you to lie to your mom and dad, he's bad news.

NICOLE: No good can come from deceit, Audra. A boy who wants you to deceive your parents from the very beginning will only ask more and more of you in the future. If you give in to him now, what's to say you won't do it again and again? By entertaining the idea, you're setting yourself up for some rough teen years of distrust and fear. It's never fun to lie to your parents—you'll walk around on eggshells, always afraid you've been caught.

I'm glad you don't feel right about it and reached out for help. You're right to have doubts about this boy, and that doesn't mean you're judging him. Only God can judge someone's sin and the condition of his heart and motives. But you can and should react to what you see right in front of you. He's giving you solid proof that he's a liar and will tempt you to lie. That's more than enough information to know you should run fast and far in the other direction.

So flee youthful passions and pursue righteousness, faith, love, and peace, along with those who call on the Lord from a pure heart.
2 TIMOTHY 2:22 ESV

PROMISES, PROMISES

I Promise

Q: *I made a promise that I don't think I should keep. Do I have to? The story is that my sixteen-year-old brother has started to do some dangerous things. He and his friends are drinking and even sometimes driving. He let me drink a beer once, which I totally regret, but really don't want my mom to know about. My brother says that if I tell my mom what he's been doing, he'll tell her that I drank a beer. At this point, I'm more worried that he's going to get hurt, but I did promise him that I'd keep his secret. What should I do?*

~MARYANNA

EMILY: If I were you, I would definitely tell your mom that your brother is drinking and driving. Maybe you can even confess what you did to your mom and let her know that you won't ever do it again instead of waiting to see if he tells. That way, she'd know that you really mean it. Worst-case scenario: What if something happened to him and you hadn't gotten him the help he needed? How would you feel? I know that if I were in that exact situation, I'd tell my mom. You might get into some trouble, but that shouldn't keep you from doing everything you can to protect your brother's life.

NICOLE: Maryanna, you're so right to be concerned. Did you know that drunk driving kills eight to ten teens every single day? The worst thing that could happen is that your brother would get hurt—or hurt someone else—and you could have done something to stop it but didn't. Seriously, don't let another day pass without having this conversation with your mom. This is a nonnegotiable decision.

My prayers are with you and your family. The girls and I prayed for your brother's safety and for wisdom for your mom in how to deal with this. Don't worry about your brother being upset with you, Maryanna. It will pass. I promise!

> *"Be on your guard! If your brother sins, rebuke him; and if he repents, forgive him."*
> LUKE 17:3 NASB

Pinkie Promise

Q: *I gave my heart to Jesus when I was a little girl. I believe in God and the Bible. But I still wonder how I can really know for sure that I am going to heaven. Sometimes I wonder if it's all a big fairy tale, and then I worry that God's upset with me for even wondering that.*

~BETH

EMILY: Do you believe that God keeps His promises? He has told you that you only need to pray to Jesus and ask Him to be your Savior to be assured you'll go to heaven. If you believe in God, then you have to believe that He doesn't lie. If He doesn't lie, then it's a done deal.

NICOLE: This is a great question and one that most Christians ask themselves at some point. Emily is right. It's a promise from God. Doubting your salvation is the same thing as doubting that He keeps His word. Whether you feel worthy or not, your salvation is a guarantee—it's not a hope-you're-good-enough kind of thing.

In Romans we're told that we simply need to confess (speak) with our mouths and believe in our hearts that Jesus is Lord, and we're saved. So we can't just say it—we must believe it. That doesn't mean that moments of doubt cancel out your salvation, but when you doubt, you should take it to God in prayer and ask Him to remove all hints of confusion.

As a caution, I'd like to add that when people begin to raise doubts like this, they often start trying to get in good with God by doing all sorts of good things. Don't fall into the trap of trying to "do" your way into heaven. There's no good you can do or bad you can do that will outweigh what Jesus did on the cross.

In hope of eternal life, which God, that cannot lie, promised before the world began.
TITUS 1:2 KJV

Keeping Your Word

Q: *Oh no! I told my mom I would babysit my little brother and sister this weekend, but I just found out that a friend is having a party. Can I get out of the babysitting job, or do I have to do it?*

~REECE

EMILY: If you told your mom you would babysit, then you should go ahead and do it. God wants you to always do what you say you're going to do and to keep your promises. It's always best to follow through with your commitments. There will always be other parties, but the faith people have in you cannot be easily replaced. But, as in anything, you should talk to your mom about it. Let her know that you're not backing out, but ask her if she has another idea or possible solution.

NICOLE: First of all, I commend you for asking. Many teens would automatically try to get out of the babysitting job in favor of the party. In fact, when I worked as a retail manager at the mall, I often had employees quit their jobs when something fun came up and they couldn't get the day off. As a mom, I would never, ever allow that, and I was shocked every time it happened.

But I'll answer as a mom who has counted on babysitters in the past and will again in the future. If it were me you were babysitting for, I would understand that you want to be with your friends and don't want to miss out on a fun night. So I would be okay with you not babysitting if you found a suitable replacement. Suitable is important—it can't be just anyone. And you'd have to find the replacement, not leave it up to me. If you couldn't achieve that, then I would expect you to honor your commitment.

> *"Don't say anything you don't mean."*
> MATTHEW 5:33 MSG

A Still, Small Voice

Q: *If God promises to answer my prayers, why don't I ever see them being answered? Some people can pinpoint direct and obvious answers to prayers, but it never happens that way for me.*

~MADISON

EMILY: You know, I've kind of had this same question. I mean, sometimes you hear these great stories about ways that God really did something big for someone. Then I realized that I am seeing those miracles—He meets all of my needs through my parents and the rest of my family. So far in my life, I don't really have the need for those major, earthshaking things to happen. He takes care of me. I guess that's miracle enough for me. How about you? Can you see God's hand in your everyday life? Maybe He wants you to find Him there first.

NICOLE: I'm thinking of one story where a couple I know needed a specific dollar amount to pay a bill they were very worried about. It was crunch time, and they needed the money immediately. They prayed together—if I remember correctly, it was for an amount like $217. They sat back and waited expectantly.

Across town, someone they knew felt led by God to drive over to their house and empty the contents of his wallet into his friends' hands. It wound up being the exact amount they needed to pay the bill. They hadn't communicated about this need, and they've all since testified that the story is true.

So it's true, sometimes God does move in big, miraculous ways to get our attention. Other times, He's only a still, small voice that moves quietly in our lives. Personally, I get a lot more of the still, small voice than I do of the blatant miracles. But either way, I can look back over my life and see God's hand of mercy and protection on me every step of the way. Take a look— bet you can see it, too.

> *After the earthquake there was a fire. But the LORD wasn't in the fire. And after the fire there was a quiet, whispering voice.*
> 1 KINGS 19:12 GW

Healer of Hurting Hearts

Q: *Things are kind of rough in my life, and people are always telling me to pray and have faith. I'm supposed to trust that God loves me and wants the best for me, but if He knows I am hurting, why doesn't He just help me?*

~Nadine

EMILY: Sometimes when those things happen, it's just a part of this life, not because God caused them to happen. He's always involved in your life, and in everything that happens, and He cares, but sometimes we just have to face the things that come our way because other people choose to do wrong. It's one way we know to look forward to heaven.

NICOLE: Yeah, Em is right. It's a shame, but this world is full of hardship, trials, and pain. It didn't have to be this way. God wanted the earth to be sinless and blissful. But sin entered, and with it came death and deterioration that brought on hardship, pain, and turmoil. He intervenes in matters of the flesh sometimes but not always. There's no way for us to fully grasp what His reasoning is, except to believe that He has a plan.

Ultimately, He does save us from the pain of this world with an eternal salvation. As followers of Christ we are guaranteed an escape. Try to be more focused on your eternal relationship with God and what that will be like, instead of looking at what God is doing in the present. Pray that He'll give you eyes to see His will and a heart of faith to trust in it.

> *"Be strong and courageous. Do not fear or be in dread of them, for it is the Lord your God who goes with you. He will not leave you or forsake you."*
> DEUTERONOMY 31:6 ESV

TECHNICALLY
SPEAKING

Cyber Stalker

Q: *My fifteen-year-old friend is constantly on the Internet talking to strangers. A seventeen-year-old guy has been talking to her every day for weeks and now he wants to meet her. He says he lives an hour away but will drive to her town. I'm worried about her and want her to either stop talking to him or tell her mom about it. She won't do either. What should I do?*

~Camry

NATALIE: I think you should keep pressuring her about this. Let her know you aren't trying to be a pain about it, but that you're really worried. If she won't stop, you should go to her mom yourself. This is nothing to mess around with because men pretend to be teenage boys to get in touch with girls all the time. Girls get killed in these situations, and I'm sure you don't want to wait until something bad happens to your friend before acting on what you know.

NICOLE: Natalie is totally right on this! Really, you don't know for sure how old he is or what he looks like. She might think she's seen a picture, but how does she know that's really a picture of him? We can't know for sure that his intentions are to hurt her, but neither can we know that they aren't. It's absolutely unsafe for a teenager to meet a stranger from the Internet.

Warning bells don't go off when a predator logs into a chat room. They look and act just like the person they want you to believe they are, and sadly, they are often successful. Girls get kidnapped, raped, sold to other countries as sex slaves, and murdered every single day by predators who found them on the Internet.

If she won't stop talking to him, you need to let her parents know immediately before it's too late.

Submit yourselves therefore to God. Resist the devil, and he will flee from you.
James 4:7 esv

Case Sensitive

Q: *My parents make me give them the passwords to everything: Facebook, e-mail, MySpace. They even check my text messages and go through my purse when I'm in the shower. So far, it hasn't bothered me all that much, but I'm fifteen now. I'd like to be able to talk to my friends without my parents looking over my shoulder. Am I being unreasonable. . .or are they?*

~KAYLA

NATALIE: I'm dealing with the same issue. My mom goes through my text messages randomly, and I'm not allowed to delete texts without handing over my phone for a quick inspection first. I have to give my passwords for everything, too. It can be annoying, but I do understand, and it was a deal I agreed to. Mom pointed out that I don't have to be allowed to text or have computer access, so if I did, those were her terms. She just wants to make sure I'm safe and protect me from any temptations that might creep in. You might feel like your parents are bugging you, but a lot of girls your age wish theirs would pay that much attention to them. Sure sounds like yours love you.

NICOLE: I'm probably the last person you want to hear from on this. I believe not only that it's *okay* for parents to check up on their teens, but that it's also their responsibility to do so. We have to do our very best to protect you from danger and from poor choices. You aren't equipped to know what to do in every situation, so your parents have to watch your back.

Be grateful they care. I promise you'll thank them one day even if it's not fun now. I promise.

> *Obey your spiritual leaders, and do what they say. Their work is to watch over your souls, and they are accountable to God.*
> HEBREWS 13:17 NLT

Let's Dance!

Q: *My friends have been making dance videos with their computers and posting them on YouTube. I want to make one, too, but I worry about who might see it. Is it okay to do it if I don't say my name or anything that identifies me?*

~EVE

EMILY: It depends a lot on what you do in the video, like what song you dance to and how you dance to it. You want to be careful about the types of movements you do and the clothes you wear, because it is a public video and it won't ever go away. Once you put it online, it's there forever. Even if you delete it one day, it's still out there.

NICOLE: You really need to do some research about online safety. Emily is very right—once you post anything, you can never fully retrieve it. You can delete it from the source, but you can't get it back from everyone else who has downloaded it or erase it from cached versions of the pages that hosted the material.

I'm not saying that YouTube is all bad—it's not. I use it myself. There's even a YouTube channel for Scenarios4Girls. But let me caution you about three things:

- Don't post anything you wouldn't want everyone in your life to see.
- Don't post anything that gives away your location, address, school, etc.
- Don't post anything without permission.

If you can post your video within those guidelines, then go for it. Just be very careful—predators are highly skilled at identifying your location from items in your room.

> *Nothing in all creation is hidden from God's sight. Everything is uncovered and laid bare before the eyes of him to whom we must give account.*
> HEBREWS 4:13 NIV

Online Dangers

Q: *My friend has been talking to a guy online and she plans to meet him in a week. I've heard all of the horror stories and know just how dangerous it can be to meet strangers from the Internet. What can I do to stop her? Or should I stay out of it because it's none of my business?*

~KERI

NATALIE: Staying out of it is not an option. You need to show your friend stories of what has happened in these kinds of cases. If she won't stop having contact with him, you need to go to her parents right away. This is a highly dangerous situation and needs to be dealt with right away.

NICOLE: This is definitely your business—it's everyone's business. We, who have knowledge and understanding of what happens, need to reach out to those who don't believe the facts or are blind to the risks they're taking. You know, if something bad happened to your friend, and statistics say it's pretty likely, you'd never forgive yourself for not getting involved.

There are a lot of things you can do. Normally I would say to talk to your friend first and give her the chance to stop the behavior before you go to an adult. But not in this case. I would be too afraid that she'd tell you she quit talking to strangers but would still be doing it without you knowing—until it was too late. You need to involve her parents. If they don't believe you or don't want to take action, you can call the police.

I know how difficult it is to go against your friend. I know you're worried about losing her friendship. Unfortunately, the choices she is making right now make all of that secondary to the real risk she is facing.

"Watch out for false prophets. They come to you in sheep's clothing, but inwardly they are ferocious wolves."
MATTHEW 7:15 NIV

Eye of the Beholder

Q: *I'm thirteen. Is it really so bad to watch R-rated movies? I mean, it's not like I'm going to act or talk like they do in the movies, and it's probably no worse than what goes on at my school.*

~GIANNA

EMILY: At thirteen, I'd have to say that it's not good for you to watch those movies because there are always things in them that you shouldn't be seeing. When I happen to see things on TV or in a movie that aren't right, it makes me feel really uncomfortable and I want to turn it off. My mom says that's the Holy Spirit showing me what's okay. I think it's important to listen to that voice.

I understand what you mean about it being no worse than what happens in your school. But just because that stuff is going on doesn't mean you should expose yourself to even more of it.

NICOLE: Well said, Emily. I'm reminded of a verse in Philippians that tells us we're to focus on and think about things that are pure and of benefit to us. We're not supposed to keep our thoughts centered on unrighteous things just because there's worse out there. Either it's godly or it's not.

An age-old part of human nature is to do as much as we can get away with and even push it past the line whenever possible—without being *too* bad. And don't get me wrong; over the course of my life, I'm guilty of the same thing. I guess I just think we would be far better off if we moved away from the middle of the road and what's "good enough" and scooted further toward righteous and godly. To do that, it's all about choices.

Flee the evil desires of youth and pursue righteousness, faith, love and peace, along with those who call on the Lord out of a pure heart.
2 TIMOTHY 2:22 NIV

Should I Stay or Should I Go?

Q: *Every time I'm online, this guy tries to talk to me. His name is Steve78. He's really nice, never says anything wrong, and listens to my problems. It's nice to have someone to talk to since I'm home alone a lot. Recently he said he wanted to meet up with me. He offered to come to a public place like the mall or a park. Should I go?*

~ALYSON

NATALIE: No way! Number one: you don't really know who he is at all. Number two: you don't know what his motives are. Why does he have no friends in real life so that he has to troll the Internet to find them? Consider that if he is always there waiting for you, he must have a pretty lonely life—which is a signal of a big problem to me.

NICOLE: Absolutely not. Alyson, I'm so very glad you wrote and didn't just go meet this guy somewhere. I find it interesting that he offered the mall and the park as two public places. The park is definitely not what I'd consider to be public, and something tells me that's where you'd have been directed to go. Do you have any idea how many teenagers just like you are lured to a "public" park under these exact same circumstances each year, then hauled off into the bushes to be raped or worse?

Listen, this guy is up to no good and you are at risk. I'd actually like for you to involve your parents before you log back on to your computer. Ask them to call the police and set up a sting operation where the police would go meet him posing as you. This happens so frequently, there are people on the police force who do this all the time. Let them handle it. If it turns out to be a mistake, then you can move on and spend more time with people your own age. But if I'm right and this guy is bad news, you'll have protected yourself and saved countless other girls from the same danger.

Listen, my son, accept what I say, and the years of your life will be many. I instruct you in the way of wisdom and lead you along straight paths. When you walk, your steps will not be hampered; when you run, you will not stumble. Hold on to instruction, do not let it go; guard it well, for it is your life.
PROVERBS 4:10–13 NIV

PURITY AND OTHER TOUGH STUFF

Never Too Late

Q: *My boyfriend and I have messed around a lot. I'm not sure if we've gone all the way, so I'm not sure if I'm actually a virgin. What exactly does it mean to lose my virginity? I wish I could go back and start over.*

~Kortnee

NATALIE: I'm not sure I get how you don't know if you've gone all the way—I'll let Mom handle that part. I can say something about starting over because I've heard my mom speak about this and I know that God is all about do-overs. If you pray for forgiveness and you commit to keeping your walk pure from now on, it is a fresh start in God's eyes.

NICOLE: Technically, virginity has to do with sexual intercourse. If you're not sure what that physically entails, you should talk to your mom about that. It's not uncommon to be unsure about virginity, though. Many times, people, teens included, get very close to actual intercourse and decide to stop, or they do everything but the actual act of intercourse and wonder if that counts.

Emotionally and spiritually, I believe virginity involves anything that requires you to surrender your heart, mind, and body to someone else in complete physical intimacy. That can be through acts other than technical intercourse.

In John 8, the Pharisees brought a woman to Jesus who had been caught in the act of cheating on her husband and demanded that, according to the law, she be stoned for what she'd done. Jesus said that any of those accusers who were without sin could cast the first stone at her. All of those men left because they knew they weren't without sin and therefore weren't worthy to condemn her. Then Jesus told her she was forgiven and to go sin no more.

That's the issue right there. In order to start over, you need to confess and then change your ways. Be forgiven of your sins by God; then go and sin no more.

If we confess our sins, He is faithful and just to forgive us our sins and to cleanse us from all unrighteousness.
1 John 1:9 NKJV

207

Blind Eye

Q: *About a week ago, I was having trouble sleeping at night, so I went to talk to my dad in his office. When I walked in, I saw some really bad things on his computer screen, but I don't think he knows I saw it. I thought it was wrong to watch that stuff. Why would my dad do that, and what should I say to him?*

~SHELBY

NATALIE: Instead of burying this and keeping it inside, you should go talk to your dad. It's possible that it was a mistake that the website opened, or maybe he clicked the wrong link, which has happened even to me, unfortunately. If you're open with him, it'll give him the chance to explain. If you keep it inside, then it will just build up and you'll always wonder about the truth.

NICOLE: Natalie, that's a fantastic point. Openness and honesty are the best things. It's entirely possible that it was an innocent error. That's the reason it's so important to be very careful when surfing the Web. You can't un-see images that pop up before your eyes. In fact, that very thing happened to me because I clicked a link in an e-mail that turned out to be porn. It was an e-mail from a trusted friend, so I thought it would be fine. Turns out, she'd been hacked. So first give him the chance to explain.

However, it may very well be that your dad was doing something wrong. Yes, pornography is sinful. That's a fact. Sometimes parents do things that even they know are wrong—they're human just like you. I'm not at all excusing your dad's choices, but I don't want you to fall for the lie that Satan wants you to believe. Satan loves to use pornography to divide families, and whether your dad was guilty or innocent, you need to get closure on this so you can move past it without it hanging over your head. Another reason you need to talk to your dad about this and be open with him about your confusion is so he can see how choices and mistakes can really affect you, and how the Internet needs to be protected in your home.

*I will set no wicked thing
before mine eyes.*
PSALM 101:3 KJV

208

In Crisis

Q: *I'm only fifteen, and I think I'm pregnant. I just know my parents are going to kill me. What should I do?*

~Jasmine

NATALIE: Tell them immediately. The longer you keep this to yourself, the harder it will be for your parents to help you through it. You're missing out on their love and support every day that you keep this from them. Your parents will not kill you. They will be disappointed and will grieve that you're going through this, but they won't kill you.

NICOLE: Oh, Jasmine. I'm so sorry that you're going through this. It's very important that you don't face it alone, though. I know you feel like your parents are going to be mad, but I promise they won't kill you. I was nineteen when I had to tell my mom and dad that I was going to be an unwed mom. I knew they'd be very disappointed, and I was right. I figured my mom would be angry; I was right. I knew they'd love me anyway and eventually come around and support me in what I faced; I was right.

Everyone makes mistakes. Yours happens to be pretty obvious to the public (or will be soon, anyway), and it carries some long-term consequences and some life-changing results. It's vital that you partner with your parents and make the best decision possible for the baby, for yourself, and even for them. Contact your local crisis pregnancy center (not Planned Parenthood) to learn about adoption or receive help if you decide to keep the baby.

It's going to be okay as things fall into place, but right now you need to confirm whether or not you truly are pregnant, and then, if you are, you need immediate prenatal care to make sure you're giving your baby everything it needs. You've got a long road ahead, but the Lord will carry you every step of the way.

> *If we confess our sins, he is faithful and just to forgive us our sins and to cleanse us from all unrighteousness.*
> 1 John 1:9 esv

Trust Your Instincts

Q: *There's a twenty-three-year-old youth worker at my church who pays extra attention to me, and it's starting to get a little weird. He texts me all the time and wants to know what I'm doing and who I'm with. Sometimes he even shows up wherever I am. At first it seemed harmless, but now, I'm not so sure. I haven't told my mom because she'd probably get upset and tell someone, and I would be so embarrassed if I were wrong. What should I do?*

~Jaime

NATALIE: I think you need to talk to your mom or dad right away. It's not okay for him to behave that way with an underage girl. He might be perfectly innocent, but you aren't the one who should verify that—it's too risky. You need to involve someone who can watch your back and make sure you're okay. In the meantime, never get in a car with him or in a situation where you're alone.

NICOLE: I agree with Natalie, but I think it goes deeper than that. So many bad things can come out of a situation like this. It's completely inappropriate for him to be paying that kind of extra attention to you, and it really makes me question what he's after.

Run—don't walk—to your mom, and show her the text messages. Tell her everything, even the things you think aren't important, and let her decide how to handle it. This is too much for you to try to handle on your own, and really, what if something bad happened? Horrible things happen every single day because of the exact scenario you've described. Don't let yourself fall victim to that when you have the chance, and clearly the wisdom, to see that something isn't quite right.

> *For sound advice is a beacon, good teaching is a light, moral discipline is a life path.*
> PROVERBS 6:23 MSG

Creeped Out

Q: *I'm fourteen and my brother is sixteen. He constantly brings his friends over when my mom isn't home, even though he's not supposed to. The worst part is that his friends are always hitting on me, and one of them really gives me the creeps and has tried to touch me. How can I tell my brother—or should I tell him?*

~KATE

NATALIE: You should definitely tell your brother that you're not comfortable with his friends in the house, especially when your mom isn't home. As his little sister, your brother should be eager to protect you and make sure you're comfortable at home. If he won't do something, you should go to your mom and let her know what's going on.

NICOLE: I'm not as worried about your brother having friends over in general. If he were here asking me the question about having friends over when he wasn't supposed to, I'd tell him not to. But that isn't my concern right now. The fact that they're hitting on you and making you uncomfortable to the point where one of them gives you the creeps—that's a problem.

Sixteen-year-old boys flirt with fourteen-year-old girls. That's natural and logical. The problem is that you're there without supervision, your parents are unaware, and one of the boys is taking it too far. I'd love more information about what happened when the creepy boy tried to touch you, but without it, I can tell you with certainty that you need to talk to your mom. You don't need to go to your brother first—in fact, I'd caution you not to. He would probably try to keep you quiet. It's necessary for your protection, and potentially the protection of other young girls, that a trusted adult be made aware of what's going on.

If they come over and your mom's not home, leave. Go to a neighbor's house, or call a friend to come pick you up—with or without permission. This is one of those times when your own safety is more important than a rule.

But their evil intentions will be exposed when the light shines on them.
EPHESIANS 5:13 NLT

211

Baby Steps

Q: *So, about in November my dad cheated on my mom, and it really hurts inside. I don't really forgive him and don't feel close to him anymore. What should I do?*

~SIANNA

NATALIE: Wow. That would be so hard! I think you should talk to a school counselor or someone you trust about how you're feeling.

Are your parents working it out and staying together? If so, I'd really encourage you to support them and try to get past your resentment if you can. Talk to your parents about how you feel, but try to forgive and not make it more stressful than it has to be. The truth is out, and nothing will be the same for a long time, but every step you take forward is one step closer to healing.

NICOLE: Oh, Sianna, I'm so sorry you have to face this. I can only imagine how you must feel. The anger, sense of betrayal, and fear of the future are very real feelings that shouldn't be ignored. I understand what Natalie is saying about not making things more stressful, but I don't want you to ignore your own needs, either. This isn't the time to clam up—you and your parents need to communicate with each other.

You also should be spending a lot of time in prayer. God knows what you're going through and He's already walking with you through it, but prayer changes your focus and helps you to surrender your control to Him.

So, communication, prayer, and then forgiveness. I think of how Jesus must feel when we walk all over the grace He's shown us by turning back to the wrong people or behaviors. That's a huge betrayal, yet He's able to forgive us over and over again. He calls us to that same level of forgiveness toward others. It's not easy, but He will help you through it. One step of faith at a time.

> *"For if you forgive other people when they sin against you, your heavenly Father will also forgive you."*
> MATTHEW 6:14 NIV

Memory of an Elephant

Q: *I recently had a friend tell me that I hold grudges too long. It's true. If someone hurts me or wrongs me, I have a really hard time getting over it. As a Christian, I know I'm supposed to forgive and forget, but how can I do that if I'm still angry?*

~Siaun

NATALIE: It can be easy to forgive, but forgetting is difficult. That final step of forgiveness doesn't mean you have to, or even can, erase your memory, but it does mean you need to let go of the negative feelings the memory causes. God calls us to show His love to others. Since He has forgiven each one of us so much, He wants us to show that same love to other people.

NICOLE: God is able to forgive and forget, but sadly, I can't. I forgive quickly and easily, but I seldom forget anything. I can't help it; I have a great memory. Do you see what I'm getting at? You can't control your memory. Forgiving someone doesn't automatically dump the event from your brain. It's part of your history—part of you—that cannot be erased from your mind unless God chooses to do it supernaturally.

The "forget" part of forgiving really has to do with trust, not forgetting. True forgiveness means you can no longer hold the event over someone's head. It means you move forward as though it never happened, and you never use it as a manipulative tool. It means you have faith that the person will try not to do it again. But, just as you're not perfect, neither is the person you're trying to forgive. That's why we're asked to forgive as many times as necessary—even seventy times seven.

> *"And when you stand praying, if you hold anything against anyone, forgive them, so that your Father in heaven may forgive you your sins."*
> MARK 11:25 NIV

Touchy Subject

Q: *What's wrong with holding hands, kissing, etc., before marriage?*

~NADIA

NATALIE: It's not the specifics of what you do; it's more about knowing your personal limits. I think the best way to judge those limits is by whether you have to hide what you're doing. You probably wouldn't have to hide it if you're holding hands with someone, but you might want to hide kissing—so, to me, that makes it wrong.

NICOLE: Well, "etc." can mean a lot of things, so I'm pretty much going to tell you to skip the "etc." part completely—until marriage, that is. As for holding hands, I personally have no problem with that for teens of appropriate dating age. For me, that's sixteen in most cases, but it's always dependent on the individual. I wouldn't condone any kind of physical contact for teens who have not yet reached that point.

Kissing. . .well, that's a touchy subject. (Get it? Touchy?) The thing is, the Bible says we aren't to lust after another person. In fact, lust is a sin. So if you're kissing someone and that leads to lust, it's sinful. How will you know where the line from a nice, romantic kiss is crossed and it becomes lustful until it actually happens?

While kissing in itself might not be technically wrong, it can lead to sin that you may or may not be able to control. You're far better off avoiding those situations. Why not commit to sharing your first kiss with your husband on your wedding day? Before you roll your eyes and decide I'm crazy, consider it. I know several people personally who have done that—just imagine how precious their weddings were, how beautiful their marriages are, and how unlikely divorce is for those couples. Just think about it.

> *So I say, walk by the Spirit,*
> *and you will not gratify*
> *the desires of the flesh.*
> GALATIANS 5:16 NIV

Just Say No!

Q: *My sixteen-year-old boyfriend wants to have sex. I don't think I'm ready, but I really don't want to lose him. What should I do?*

~CAITLIN

NATALIE: Say no. Think about your future and all of the wonderful things God has planned for you if you follow His will. Don't trade that in for a temporary thing just to please someone else who isn't going to be around forever. I'm fully committed to waiting until marriage, and I'm praying for my husband now. This puts my mind on the future rather than on today, and it helps me make better decisions now. Turn your focus to what God has planned for your future and settle for nothing less for yourself than His perfect blessings.

NICOLE: Look at all of the women you know ranging from eighteen to seventy. Take a poll. How many of them are still with the boy they dated when they were sixteen? It's going to be an extremely low percentage. Extremely low. By the nature of statistics, the likelihood you'll still be dating this boy in a year (especially when you think not having sex with him might push him away) is slim.

What does that have to do with sex? Everything! If you give your purity to this boy because you hope to keep him around, you'll find yourself alone and full of regrets. Some things can't be undone, and sex is one of them. You will remember your sexual experiences for the rest of your life. If you think you need to have sex with this boy to keep him, what about the next one? With that mind-set, how many sexual partners will you have before you marry?

Past sexual experiences and partners cause huge problems in marriage. Those physical bonds exist forever, and there's no erasing the actions or the memories. That truth is like a dark cloud over the covenantal relationship you will make between yourself, your husband, and God.

It's not worth it. Trust me.

I highly recommend you pick up my book *Swept Away* and read Lilly's story.

> *Don't let sin rule your body. After all, your body is bound to die, so don't obey its desires or let any part of it become a slave of evil.*
> ROMANS 6:12–13 CEV

Cutting Edge

Q: *My sister is sixteen, and I'm fourteen. Recently, I noticed a bunch of cuts on her arms. What are they from, and what should I do about it?*

~BRITTANY

NATALIE: Most likely your sister is cutting. Sadly, cutting is very common. I see it all the time in my school. It's really a cry for help. People in this situation are usually feeling a lot of stress and pressure. You definitely need to confide in someone you trust who can reach out to your sister and help her through whatever she's feeling. You should also talk to her and let her know you notice what's going on and that you care about her.

NICOLE: It's really difficult to understand why someone would hurt herself on purpose. Sometimes teens do this because their emotional hurt is so strong, they'd rather feel physical pain. This behavior is always a sign that something is wrong. Usually people who do this haven't figured out other ways to handle tough things and pain.

Sometimes traumatic experiences like the loss of a loved one, a breakup, a divorce in the family, abuse, etc., can cause teens to feel numb. The pain experienced through cutting and other forms of self-injury can be a way to wake up from that numbness—but they usually don't realize that's why they're doing it. That's why it's so hard to stop without professional help.

Cutters need to recognize what's driving their behavior and find other ways to meet those needs before they're able to stop. They need to replace this unhealthy coping mechanism with a healthy one.

At this point, you need to take this information to a parent. Someone with the ability to get your sister help needs to be involved. This is way too much for you to handle on your own, even if your sister says she has it under control. Since cutting often leads to bigger things, don't wait another day before going after help for her.

Do you not know that your body is a temple of the Holy Spirit within you, whom you have from God? You are not your own, for you were bought with a price. So glorify God in your body.
1 CORINTHIANS 6:19–20 ESV

Safety Net

Q: *My school passes out condoms to anyone who wants them. I used to think that was horrible, but lately I've been thinking I should get one and keep it in my purse—just in case. What do you think?*

~Gina

NATALIE: I think that by giving yourself a safety net, you're opening the door for the possibility of giving in to temptation in the heat of the moment. It would be much better to be strong and sure of your commitment to God's will, which asks you to live in purity until marriage. If you're committed to that, you need the Holy Spirit to help you in times of temptation, not a condom.

NICOLE: Yep. You'd be much less likely to jump from a window unless you saw a net below. Protect your commitment by supporting the choice to say no, not providing yourself the means to fail.

There's a big debate in religion and politics about even allowing condoms or other forms of birth control to be passed out in schools. Most religious circles would agree with what I said above. Political debates span both sides. Many people don't have a stance on the issue of teens and birth control but still don't believe the schools should meddle in that subject at all.

Because of all of that confusion out there, I'm going to recommend that you talk to your parents about this one. If you don't feel like that's possible, what about a youth pastor or youth leader at church? This is a very serious subject. Condoms and other forms of birth control are basically just an open door to sin.

> *Don't become like the people of this world. Instead, change the way you think. Then you will always be able to determine what God really wants—what is good, pleasing, and perfect.*
> ROMANS 12:2 GW

217

A Pure Start

Q: *I've already had sex with someone. We're not together anymore, and I guess I'm kind of like damaged goods. Since I've already done it, what's the point of trying not to from now on?*

~DAKOTA

NATALIE: In my mom's book *Essence of Lilly*, which you can find in the two-in-one *Swept Away*, Lilly visited a counseling group where girls were all in that situation. The counselor helped them work through their guilt and regret and led them to reclaim their purity. Spiritual purity is more important than physical purity, and God can heal your heart and restore your mind and body to a place where you don't feel damaged any longer.

NICOLE: Oh, wow. This is a huge trap. It's a lie from Satan, actually. He wants you to believe you're dirty, damaged, and unworthy. He wants you to seek attention from boys through physical acts by making you think that's the only way you can get it. He wants you to think that God is angry with you and that you've cheated yourself out of the best future possible by giving yourself away at a young age. Am I right?

Okay, this is the moment of transition. This is the moment when you say, "*No more!*" Be done with those lies and those feelings of being used or damaged. If you haven't yet, seek forgiveness from God for your choices, and ask the Holy Spirit to heal your heart. Then let it go. I know the memories are there, and the feelings don't go away that easily, but you need to grab hold of them and push the doubts aside. You've been made new in Christ, and no lie from your enemy can take that away from you.

> *Therefore, if anyone is in Christ, he is a new creation. The old has passed away; behold, the new has come.*
> 2 CORINTHIANS 5:17 ESV

The First Time

Q: *My boyfriend hit me—but only once. I broke up with him, but I'm thinking about getting back together with him. He's always saying he's sorry, and I really believe he is. Plus, I love him. What should I do?*

~Ivy

NATALIE: I don't think it's good at all if a guy hits a girl. If he doesn't respect you enough to keep his cool now, and takes his anger out on you physically once, he can do it again. You want someone who will treat you right, respect your thoughts and feelings, and protect you—not hurt you!

NICOLE: I love that your first response was to dump the jerk, but I'm sad that you're having doubts about your choice.

Would you believe that a full 80 percent of teen girls who have been abused in a dating relationship continue to date the abuser? Even if it was only one time, it's a mistake to believe that you haven't been abused. This mind-set is what keeps girls going back for more again and again.

First of all, no human being should hit another as a means of control or power. In a dating relationship, you should feel protected, cherished, honored—not frightened and timid. Even if he never hit you again, could you truly forget how you felt when he did? Could you ever fully trust your safety?

Secondly, girls often go back to their abusers because they want to fix the situation. They subconsciously want to prove to themselves and their abusers that they are good enough, that they can do it right and not do something to deserve being hit again. They're trying to find healing for the abuse by hoping it doesn't happen again. It will happen again.

I'm sorry to say this, Ivy, but this wasn't the *only* time; it was simply the *first* time.

> *The LORD examines the righteous, but the wicked, those who love violence, he hates with a passion.*
> PSALM 11:5 NIV

Beautiful Bird

Q: *I think I was sexually abused, but I'm not sure. What is sexual abuse, and what can I do to stop the pain I'm feeling now? Will I ever get over this feeling of worthlessness?*

~Kimmie

NATALIE: God loves you so much. He hurts when you hurt, and He wants to carry your pain. I think you need some people praying with you and for you about this. It's a big burden to carry, especially since you aren't really sure of what happened or what it all means. I do know that God is capable to get you through this and then use you one day to help other people who might have gone through the same thing. How awesome it will be to be able to be used by God!

NICOLE: Okay, first of all, the easiest way to define sexual abuse is any physical activity performed by one person without the agreement of the other. That's a good definition when it comes to adults. Now when you add children or teens into the equation, it's a whole different thing. Even if the young person agrees to the physical, sexual activity, it is still considered abuse because, as a minor, that person cannot make a sound decision about this. And anytime an adult has sex or engages in sexual activity with a minor, it is abuse. No matter what.

Have you talked to someone about this? A good counselor (be sure it's a Christian counselor) could help you uncover the truth in your past and then work through the feelings you're having. In the meantime, spend a lot of time reading in your Bible about how God feels about you and praying that you would feel that way about yourself.

Yes, you can and will get past your feelings if you surrender them to God. I'm not saying that you won't forever be affected by the abuse in your past—it's part of what has shaped who you are. But beauty can rise up from ashes. Pray that God turns your pain into compassion for others, your fear into wisdom, and your bitterness into forgiveness.

And we know that God causes everything to work together for the good of those who love God and are called according to his purpose for them.
ROMANS 8:28 NLT

Revenge Is the Lord's

Q: *Is God punishing me by allowing my friend to die because of a drunk driver? Is it wrong to hope God really punishes that man?*

~TAYLOR

NATALIE: I recently read *The Shack* in which a little girl is kidnapped and murdered. Her dad goes on a quest to come to terms with her death and realizes along the way that he must forgive. When I read this story, I struggled with the idea that God would allow something like this, but I've realized that since we have free will, sometimes bad things are simply going to happen.

NICOLE: God's heart is so grieved by the death of your friend. He suffers with you and with your friend's family as you face this horrible loss. He also grieves with and comforts the person who was at fault in this accident. It's a horrendous thing to accidentally cause the death of someone else, and that driver's life is forever changed by those actions.

There's enough education out there that you'd think people would be aware enough of the dangers that they wouldn't drink and drive, yet it persists. I guess it's the same as any sin, though. We know what we're supposed to do, and we have all of the education and resources available to help us do it, yet sometimes we still choose the sinful route.

You, having been shown grace and forgiveness to cover your own sin, now must reach deep into your soul and find the grace and mercy to forgive this drunk driver. It's a terrible tragedy, and the punishment began the moment that driver realized what had happened, and perhaps God will choose to take that punishment further. But that's for Him to decide, not you. You need to surrender your feelings of anger and rage against the driver and let God handle things from here.

Again, I am so very sorry for your loss.

> *"You shall not take vengeance, nor bear any grudge against the sons of your people, but you shall love your neighbor as yourself; I am the LORD."*
> LEVITICUS 19:18 NASB

Shine, Jesus, Shine

Q: *My mom is divorced and she's always having guys spend the night at our house. They sleep in her bedroom with her. As a Christian, I have a problem with this, but I can't get my mom to see the truth. She thinks that she's an adult making adult decisions and I should leave her alone about it. Do you think it's okay that she does that? If not, what should I do about it?*

~LINDSEY

NATALIE: I know this is your mom, but you still shouldn't pretend that something is right when it's clearly wrong. All you can do is let your mom know how you feel, but don't become disrespectful. It's very important that you pray that God would make her see that what she's doing is wrong and is setting a bad example for you. Until that happens, just keep on loving her and praying for her.

NICOLE: Oh dear. I'm sorry you have to watch this go on right in front of you, but I'm so glad you are fighting through the sin and pointing your mom to truth. First, I want to encourage you to guard your heart and mind. Fight against your enemy who is working overtime in this situation to get you to soften in your approach to sin. Satan wants nothing more than for you to weaken your resolve and welcome sin into your own life. Pray every day that the Holy Spirit would guard your heart and mind against Satan's lies.

Now, about your mom. This is going to sound strange, but I'm going to go out on a limb and tell you not to worry so much about what she's doing. Focus your concerns and prayers on why she's doing it. What's going on in her heart that makes it okay for her to act like this in front of you? How is her relationship with God? That's where your prayer focus should be. If she got her heart in line with God's will, the sin would naturally fall away because she'd grow uncomfortable with it. That's the ultimate goal!

Let your conversation be gracious and attractive so that you will have the right response for everyone.
COLOSSIANS 4:6 NLT

Peace of God

Q: *My mom died of cancer last year after battling the disease for four years. I miss her a lot, and now I'm so scared. I'm afraid that my dad will die and I'll be alone, or that I'll die. How can I get past my fear?*

~LAURA

EMILY: I'm really sorry that you lost your mom. That has to be awful! It's hard at any age to face something like that, but as a teenager, it has to be horrible.

I think it's really important that you be with people who love you and who will help you keep your mind off things. Spend time with your friends and your dad. Be sure to talk about how you feel so you can heal from the hurt. When you're afraid, pray that God would help you see that He is holding you and will protect you.

NICOLE: I'm so very sorry about your loss, Laura. I'm sure you're feeling an entire range of emotions, one of which, naturally, is fear. I hope you do have people in your life with whom you can talk about your feelings. Have you seen a counselor or talked with a pastor? You see, fear is not from God. He desires that you rest in Him and put all of your worries on His shoulders so He can carry them for you.

He has your future all worked out already—and your eternity is secure in Him. When you truly rest in that fact, the concerns of this world fade into the background. It's not that the trials and pains of life don't affect you or that you don't feel grief; it's just that those earthly things become dim in the light of God's presence in your life and the promise of eternal glory.

Again, please talk to people who can guide you spiritually as well as emotionally, and be there for your family. You're all in my prayers!

Do not be anxious about anything, but in everything by prayer and supplication with thanksgiving let your requests be made known to God. And the peace of God, which surpasses all understanding, will guard your hearts and your minds in Christ Jesus.
PHILIPPIANS 4:6–7 ESV

About the Authors

Emily Balnius is a straight-A fifth grader at Eastlawn School in Paxton, Illinois. She lives with her mom, stepdad, three sisters, and two brothers. Never found without her iPod, Emily loves to dance and sing. She's a busy girl who enjoys swimming, skateboarding, and hanging out with friends. She's active in her community and local church, and plans to be a teacher when she grows up.

Natalie Balnius is an honor student in the eighth grade at PBL Middle School in Paxton, Illinois. The oldest daughter of six kids, Natalie is a very loving and hands-on big sister. She's passionate about her walk with Christ, and almost as passionate about the game of volleyball. She holds first-chair clarinet in the school band and looks forward to high school marching band. At this point, Natalie aspires to a career in the culinary arts, but is open to other possibilities.

Nicole O'Dell has six children ranging from nineteen down to three-year-old triplets. The author of the popular Scenarios interactive fiction series for girls, Nicole writes fiction and nonfiction focused on helping teens make good choices and bridging the gap in parent/teen communication. Nicole is also the host of Teen Talk Radio at www.choicesradio.com, where she talks with teens and special guests about the real issues young people face today, and she loves getting out among teens and parents when speaking at youth groups and conferences. Visit www.nicoleodell.com and www.choose-now.com/girltalk to participate in the *Choices! Community* and learn more about the valuable resources offered by Nicole O'Dell.